ACKNOWLEDGMENTS

D1325232

I am a literary agent, and in my work, I am privileged to meet a wide variety of people. One of my favorite clients, who is also a close friend, is Dr. Anne Wilson Schaef, the well-known best-selling author of such ground-breaking books as *Women's Reality, When Society Becomes an Addict* (with Diane Fassel), *Escape from Intimacy,* and her most current bestseller, *Meditations for Women Who Do Too Much.* It's no secret that Dr. Schaef's book gave rise to this one. Moreover, Anne's body of work has had a profound effect on me and millions of others. For that I thank her.

Other important voices in the recovery and wellness movement have been important to me. They include Melody Beattie, Tom Grady, Clayton Carlson, Diane Fassel, Toni Burbank, Karen Elliot, Pat Benson, Terry Spohn, John Small, Pat Carnes, John Bradshaw, Wayne Kritsberg, Ken Dychtwald, Natalie Goldberg, Kate Green, Earnie Larsen, Carol Hegarty, the folks at

Narada, Louie Anderson, Ellen Sue Stern, Al Franken, Christina Baldwin, Joy Houghton, Robert Cooper, Harold Bloomfield, John Driggs, Steve Finn, Ruth Humleker, Bob Larranga, Alan Loy McGinnis, Gary Paulsen, Paula Nelson, Cynthia Orange, Beth Wilson Saveedra, R. D. Zimmerman, Jan Johnson, and the folks at CompCare.

A special thanks to Elizabeth Perle, who, when she was publisher of Prentice Hall Press, bought this book. Additional thanks with admiration to Marilyn Abraham, a wonderful editor with a terrific sense of humor (a redundancy), and Sheila Curry for her insight and hard work.

The people with whom I'm lucky enough to work are constant sources of pleasure and support. They include Jennifer Flannery, Amanda Steiner, Debbie Orenstein, Bonnie Blodgett, Jack Caravela, Peggy Kelly, and Mary Meehan.

Thanks for inspiration through friendship goes to Evelyn Friedberg.

Thanks to my parents, Jon and Virginia Lazear, for their lifelong interest, support, and love.

A last thank you goes to my wife, Wendy Broad Lazear, who was patient during the project, supportive, and helpful every step of the way. Our children, Michael and Ross, were patient, too, and *interested* in what Dad was doing.

JONATHON LAZEAR
Minneapolis, February 1992

INTRODUCTION

.~~.

It is with great pride and immense pleasure that I sit down to write an introduction to this book. Rarely does one have the opportunity in some small way to give back to someone who has so freely given to them. Jonathon Lazear is not only my agent, serving me beyond the call of duty in that capacity, he is my friend, my confidant, my mentor and teacher, my support and my gadfly when I need one to nip at my heels.

When Jonathon first mentioned thinking about such a book, I was delighted! My book, *Meditations for Women Who Do Too Much,* has obviously struck a nerve in a world where women have a desperate yearning to stop and take a look at *what* we are doing and the *way* we are doing it, which is often not only *not* life enhancing but destructive to ourselves, our families, our work, and our planet. Many men read *Meditations for Women Who Do Too Much* daily and I agreed with

Jonathon that there needed to be a companion volume that came from a man and spoke directly to men about the unique issues that men face in their lives. Jonathon and his book have done that.

The quotes in this book are wonderful! Having become a mini-expert on quotes, I am thrilled to say that most were new to me and are powerful and to the point. Rarely have I seen such a rich and delicious variety of memorable quotes. *And* they are used beautifully to lead into exquisite tidbits of thought-provoking and soul-stirring words for daily reflection.

I am glad the men I know will have the possibility of this little book in their lives and I am glad that I will have a new gift item that can offer doors of options from the self-abuse and self-destructive patterns I see lived out in many of the men for whom I care a great deal.

May we as men and women find new, full, life-enhancing ways to live with ourselves, with each other, and with our planet.

ANNE WILSON SCHAEF, PH.D.
AUTHOR OF *Meditations for Women Who Do Too Much*

By letting go, it all gets done;
The world is won by those who let it go!
  —THE TAO TE CHING

That is what so much of our compulsion is about; it is not "natural" for men in this age, in this society, to "let go." We hold on to old models of success, and sometimes to disastrous ways of seeing things to fruition. How often have we clung to what we thought was the life raft of sanity, of our work, of our need to complete a task, for the sake of the task, not for what it brings us.

It will be important for me to keep my real goals in perspective today. I will need to be mindful of what makes me and those I love happy, not just what keeps me occupied.

*Damn the great executives, the men of measured
merriment, damn the men with careful smiles. . . .*
  —SINCLAIR LEWIS

In our lives, beginning in childhood, we learn to
measure everything. Quantify happiness, measure accomplishment, and meter work, preferably billing by
the hour. I do not know if it is strictly a male trait to
measure work and dole out pleasure, but now I do
know that all men I once wanted to emulate were
men who had careful smiles, and used them as tech-
niques rather than honest and spontaneous reactions
to pleasure.

∼·

I want to begin to see myself as a man who doesn't
excuse pleasure, but one who seeks it out and man-
ages to bring it to my work.

Next week there can't be any crisis. My schedule is already full. —HENRY KISSINGER

Have you ever felt this way? There was a time, and it wasn't very long ago, that I would look at my schedule, a week in advance, and revel in the fact that there were few formal meetings set. As the days went by, I would always add more meetings until the weekend prior to the week ahead left me with dread because I had so overbooked myself—and all with the very best of intentions. Always taking on too much, I thereby created crisis.

.~.

Today I will listen to my heartbeat—literally. And I will let that cadence set the tone for the pace of my work.

One's action ought to come out of an achieved stillness;
not to be a mere rushing on. —D. H. LAWRENCE

A flurry of activity usually looks like work; it most often announces that a great deal is being dealt with, a genius at work, a man who knows how to stir things up to get things done. It is so terribly difficult to be quiet. Especially if you're a man who has been taught that work is noisy, physically and emotionally demanding, thankless, and of course, endless.

So much clarity of thought comes from solitude, from being undisturbed, from closing doors gently and quietly. Once I heard the voice of one of my children very clearly, after he had been asleep for a long time. I heard his voice so clearly because I allowed myself to hear it.

I need to be quiet, to listen, to stop. I will accomplish an inner harmony if I do not drown out the notes that come from within.

I think in every country that there is at least one
executive who is scared of going crazy.
—JOSEPH HELLER

I feel so worn down from trying so hard. I think so
many men like me are exhausted from being frantic.
We attempt to work on our overcommitment, our
overwork, but even that takes a new kind of toll on
us. Even the effort to become "sane" and to give
ourselves balance can leave us drained; nearly as
drained as the old obsessive work-'til-you-drop routine.

This problem of fear, of perhaps "going crazy," is
not limited to my socioeconomic peer group. It is
universal; it is worldwide; it is pervasive, persuasive,
and about as frightening as anything any man can
think of.

～

Today I will begin to understand how far-reaching
my work anxiety is. I may not beat the anxiety today,
but I will begin to understand how many of my peers
also suffer from it.

My formula for living is quite simple. I get up in the morning and I go to bed at night. In between, I occupy myself as best I can. —CARY GRANT

I wonder how often I've known only the moment of being awake, and the minute prior to drifting off at night, to be the only "absolutes" in my day. If I were spontaneous, enjoying chance, and not mindful of my need for "business," I would fill my head with an orderly and forceful view of the tasks that are before me each day.

More often than not, my days are a jumble of activity, often mindless "business"—predominantly a flurry of things half done, rarely fully accomplished. I'd really rather measure my days by virtue of the richness and variety they offer, not by how quickly they pass.

～

Today I will pause a number of times, not to look at the clock but to take a short walk or stare out the window and think about how I can be more satisfied.

The tragedy of life is what dies inside a man while he lives. —ALBERT EINSTEIN

How do we learn to keep alive those things that are important to us, those things that need to survive a busy day, a schedule crammed with things to do, endless meetings, useless activities? How often do we learn the difference between what is "important" and what can be dismissed? And what part of us dies when we make the decision to be consumed with activity rather than thought, or with "getting there" just so we could say we *were* there. Men have been taught that they must always move; frenetic activity is the physical evidence of men who do too much.

~·

I want to be aware today of what I have inside that is important. I will care less for what I "produce" and attach less importance to the evidence of being a good or prosperous man.

Always do one thing less than you think you can do.
—BERNARD BARUCH

Like most men, my eyes are bigger than my appetite.
I often give myself a very large menu of things to do,
and every morning I'm eager to get to *all* of it.
Bernard Baruch's thought speaks to measuring out
our tasks so that we do not become enslaved by
them. He suggests that we do less, because, as we've
been told over and over, very often *less is more*. Accomplishing task after task after task is not in anyone's best interest. Think about being the seventh or
twelfth patient on a surgeon's list of "things to do
today," and suddenly you get the picture. Unless it's
an emergency, I'll wait my turn.

.~.

Today I will attempt to finish something I've already
started. I will remember that seeing something
through to its completion can be more satisfying than
taking on something new.

Wisdom is knowing when you can't be wise.
—PAUL ENGLE

Change. Move. Alter. Perfect. Rearrange. Keep moving. So many of us put a lid on our wisdom by rarely, if ever, taking the time to reflect on our strengths. It takes a new method of thought and of inner patience to begin to be straight with ourselves about what we can and cannot do. When is it better for me *not* to be involved, *not* to make a decision, *not* to take a stand? I cannot always come up with an answer. Often I cannot deliver a question. Often I will be better off if I do neither.

Today I will be mindful of my limitations, and take comfort in the fact that I do not know everything, never will, and will not have to take responsibility for knowledge I do not have.

JANUARY 10

Bring over one of your old Motown records,
put the speakers in the window;
we'll go up on the roof and listen to the Miracles
echo in the alley down below   —ROD STEWART

Remember those old songs, the ones we listened to and that meant so much to us, the songs that set the stage for our first romantic experience, our winning seasons on the football fields and baseball diamonds? Whether it was the Beatles, Glen Miller, Roger Miller, or the Miracles, it's music that is often the catalyst for our memories.

Maybe it's time to dust off the old albums and listen to some of the old songs—static, dust, cracks, and all—that take us back to our more carefree thoughts and moments. Our old music can bring us back to being the boys of summer, and that would be a great way to spend just about any afternoon.

～

If there's a rhythm to our work, there's also rhythm to our memory, and many of our memories give us peace. Today I'll let some old favorites play out in my imagination, and maybe later I'll get out the old 45's.

*Four out of five people are more in need of rest than
exercise.* —DR. LOGAN CLENDENING

It is important to keep one's body in relatively good
shape. And it's been proven that certain kinds of
activities actually help alleviate some amount of
stress. But it is very dangerous to feel driven to
exercise, to run as fast and as far as you can, to be
obsessed, and yes, even addicted to it. So many of us
need to learn how to rest and when to rest; when to
work, and when to engage in physical activity.

If you think that you must always find time in
every day to do your push-ups you may just be
setting yourself up for another form of overindul-
gence. And your vanity may be winning over your
common sense.

·~·

Today I will try to find time to rest; to give my heart
and my head time to recoup. I will not feel that my
idle arms and legs betray me.

It's the hardest thing in the world to accept a little
success and leave it that way.
—MARLON BRANDO

Greed, on its many levels and in its many guises, can
be found in just about any of us, and it surfaces in
many ways. If we are just out for the last dime we
can squeeze out of a day's work, we may be secretly
disappointed in the outcome of our efforts: too much
work, too little reward. Then, next time out, we're
driving ourselves even further, desperate for the result to match the effort.

We need to begin to see our success incremen-
tally. Success usually doesn't come in megadoses. It's
the small rewards that we need to recognize and life's
little triumphs we must claim.

⌇

I will be pleased with what I accomplish today and
be mindful of my goals, but not overshadowed by
them. I will recognize the way in which greed can
undermine ambition.

Wealth is not his who has it, but his who enjoys it.
—BENJAMIN FRANKLIN

Acquisition. Ownership. Public display of wealth. These are words and concepts that speak to the man who has made it but doesn't really know what to do with it. The king is in the countinghouse, counting out his money. It's a lonely picture.

Great wealth for the sake of great wealth is an indication of a bankrupt man. We have been so caught up in acquisition that we do not know what to do with what we acquire, nor why we have it.

We are gluttons—men with endless appetites for the window dressing that proves our wholeness.

～

I will look to the people in my life who give me the wealth of kindness and understanding rather than to the things I've acquired over the time I spent filling my life with possessions.

Run, if you like, but try to keep your breath;
Work like a man, but don't be worked to death.
  —DR. OLIVER WENDELL HOLMES, SR.

If some of us are driven to fill our days with work, with accomplishments, with meetings, exchanges of one kind or another, we need to apportion those hours with time for our children, our lovers, our thoughts, our hobbies, our true selves.

It's not that there's anything wrong with being "busy," but there's plenty wrong with being "busy" just for the sake of taking up time. Being "busy" is often a smokescreen, something to hide behind. But what are we hiding from? If we stopped being "busy," what might we have to face?

∾

Today I'll try to keep in mind why I'm busy, and I'll do my best not to kick up dust just to look busy. There's too much of great and wonderful interest to fake involvement.

When did it become necessary to fill the house and office with small appliances? I've lost count of my conveniences—it's all just too much. I don't know if I have more telephone lines or television outlets, but I do know that I'm responsible for the brownout in the neighborhood. —JONATHON LAZEAR

The eighties were unkind to all of us. Many of us got caught up in making ends meet ridiculous conclusions. Always more. Never enough. The definition of the quality of life was being continuously redefined.

Now it's the nineties. And we all know what we knew all along—that the quality of life is best measured by the time spent reading a bedtime story to our four-year-old and by the expression on his face when he can't stop talking about it. Or by the time spent getting up early for our daughter's nine A.M. gymnastics meet on a wintry Saturday morning.

They could care less if they're driven to their games in a Mercedes. It's the games they're looking forward to. It's their father they're proud to be with.

~.

Today I will make a list of the things I consider necessities. I will notice how many of my possessions I can easily do without and reflect upon the meaning of "quality of life."

No grand idea was ever born in a conference, but a lot of foolish ideas have died there.
  —F. SCOTT FITZGERALD

Well, yes and no. It usually takes one man or woman to come up with the brilliant idea, and several men and women to dilute it, dissect it, misunderstand it, misjudge it, and come to the wrong conclusion about it.

Collective intellect is a contradiction in terms. Not only have foolish ideas perished but a lot of wonderful, original, creative, even offbeat ideas have died by the committee's unanimous assassination.

We put so much energy into attempting to convey our ideas, acting as cheerleaders to a group of brain-dead fans in the bleachers, that I've often thought that all the best, most important ideas die not by exposure, but because they're privately maintained in our personal wine cellars.

⋅∾⋅

Too much of my attention and energy is going toward winning the approval of the group. I'll begin to store my energies and direct them to the man or woman who can give me the nurturing feedback I need.

Man's main task in life is to give birth to himself, to become what he potentially is. The most important product of his effort is his own personality.
  —ERICH FROMM

We are often so locked up in what we think we should be, in what we think we should be doing. Erich Fromm talks about "potential," which implies growth and process, not a static, unchanging self-image. We need to be aware of "becoming," welcome and question our self-image, and accept change as inevitable and healthy.

.~.

If I miss my mark today, I will not be defeated. I will understand that life is process and that I can continuously give birth to myself.

Get in, get into the place that's your nature, whether it's running a corporation or picking daisies in the field, get in there and live to it, live to the fullness of it, become what you are, and I'll say to you, you've done more than most men. Most men . . . most of them don't ever do that. They'll work at a job and not know why. They'll marry a woman and not know why. They'll go to their graves and not know why. —E. L. DOCTOROW

What Ed Doctorow is saying is so important. He's talking about trusting ourselves, our inner core, and allowing our passion to rise and bloom.

So often we're on "automatic," getting to our job, getting through our day, making it home, to start all over, to make sure we've covered our bases, paid the mortgage, made it to the bank on time.

Doctorow wants us to dream, and allow our dreams to lead us. Like the main character in the film *Field of Dreams*, get out there, mow down the corn, and put a baseball field in our backyards. Get out there and do whatever it is we're meant to do. Live our own lives, "live to the fullness."

.~.

Today I'll begin to trust my dreams, and maybe even hear them for the first time.

No problem is too big to run away from.
  —AL RIES AND JACK TROUT

While Ries and Trout's quote is funny, it still gives rise to some contemplation. For those of us men who are overcommitted, often it seems as if all our problems are of the same magnitude. Fantasizing about running away is a sign of being in over our heads.

.~.

Today I'll look at problems that arise with a cold eye, not overreact, not enlarge upon them, and not create mountains out of molehills. I'll start with the smallest problems first and tackle the bigger problems later.

Do not on any account attempt to write on both sides of the paper at once. —W. C. SELLER

If we could, we would.

I've known work addicts whose minds are racing away. They're at their computers, typing madly, complaining that the keyboard cannot keep up with their thoughts. They're driving their secretaries to record their words at Olympian speed, becoming irritated if the pace isn't matched.

I'm not suggesting that these workers are not bright, able people, but they seem to mix up speed with quality of thought.

·~·

My pace is not yours, and I should not inflict mine on you. I will be aware of my demands and my boundaries in the future.

Now that it's all over, what did you really do yesterday that was worth mentioning? —COLEMAN COX

What is worth our time? Maybe what is most worth our time is the time we spent yesterday being quietly introspective, going within. Most of us need tangible proof, external evidence, of our productivity and our self-worth. We're so geared to the physical manifestations of our accomplishments, we often lose track of our inner voice, of the place down deep that houses what is really important to us.

Now most of us would come up empty-handed to Coleman Cox's question. And that's sad, because the ten minutes I spent with my elder son yesterday was very much worth mentioning, if only as a memory shown in my private movie theater.

.~.

Even at the risk of measuring my days in an artificial way, I want to take a few moments this evening, and every evening, to think about what I did or said that was truly important to me.

*If you don't get everything you want, think of the things
you don't get that you don't want.*
—OSCAR WILDE

Men tend, I think—more than women—to get
bound up in wanting "things." I'm not talking about
the proverbial roof over our heads, or a few good
suits, or even a car that can be counted on to start
when you turn the key. I mean big things: The BMW,
the Big Vacation Home at the Lake, the Armani
Suits, the Platinum Card. And what if we fill our lives
and every corner of our houses with these things? It
still doesn't save us from finally, one day, confronting
ourselves in what all the accumulated stuff really
means to us.

And, of course, as usual, Oscar Wilde was right.
We need to step back when we can't make a big
enough downpayment for the Maserati and say:
"Well, the roof hasn't fallen in, my kids are healthy,
and I'm really pretty happy with the old Honda."

∿

I will try to think about what kinds of things I really
need as opposed to what kinds of things I think I
deserve. I will try to concentrate more on filling my
life with things that can stand the test of time.

To do great work a man must be very idle as well as very industrious. —SAMUEL BUTLER

You look at your watch and notice you're a half hour late for the next meeting. You excuse yourself, run from the building, hail a cab, try to catch your breath, get fresh and ready for the next session. You get through it. The day is over, and you wonder if you did your best work. You think back to all the meetings, the lunches, the phone calls, and try to remember what you said. Were you good? Or did you just get by?

I have learned, and it's been a hard lesson, that the more time I take to be still, sometimes introspective, or just to catch my breath, the better my next task is completed. I get better results when I make the pauses as meaningful as the battle.

Clear, logical, unencumbered thinking is done without distraction. And we must never let ourselves think that distractions cause us to be sharper, better thinkers.

.~.

I must learn to put as much of my concentration into my idle moments as I do into my "productive" ones. I must learn the usefulness of punctuating my day with pauses.

Perhaps the best thing about the future is that it only comes one day at a time. —DEAN ACHESON

It is pleasant to think about the spring, especially if you're currently shoveling twelve inches of snow from the driveway. But what about today? We seldom give ourselves up to the moment and allow ourselves to experience and enjoy what is happening today.

We must learn to anticipate positive thoughts in a different, gentler light. The future is in five minutes as well as next April or next year. Today is yesterday's future, and we must set our inner "expectation clocks" back from time to time. Frantically planning ahead only works if your days are devoid of happiness and serenity.

~

Each day I need to think about the future, but in smaller increments. Today, truly, is the future.

The great secret of success is to go through life as man who never gets used up. —ALBERT SCHWEITZER

So often, by about five P.M., most of us feel used up. We're running on empty by midday. At five o'clock we stumble to our cars or to the subway and barely notice the trip home.

How can we change this? One way is to know the signs of impending exhaustion. We need to be vigilant about how far we stretch ourselves, and we can only do that when we begin to stop taking on too much responsibility. Often we think about men who are described as pillars of their communities because they're on the parks commission, teach Sunday school, coach Little League, and cross the finish line at the town marathon.

I find a man who fits that description just a bit suspect. He's in over his head, most often by choice, and he's the man who will, someday, get "used up."

∾

I need to recognize my own personal limits so that what I do take on I enjoy. I need to remember that I can't get the toothpaste back into the tube.

A ten thousand-aspirin job.
—JAPANESE SAYING FOR
EXECUTIVE RESPONSIBILITY

Work. What do we make of it? What does it give
back to us? Are the terms *career* and *work* synonymous? Should they be?

Work for work's sake. Activity. Obsession. The
Japanese have no corner on the workaholic market,
but they do have a phrase for it, and they're beginning to understand that it is killing many men.

We must examine why we work, what our work
is, and if it gives us any pleasure. How much are we
willing to sacrifice so that we can make the mortgage
payment?

⌇

I will examine why I'm working at this job, and I will
think about how I can not enslave myself to my job.
I will also think about play, and how to incorporate
play into my everyday life.

There is an obvious cure for failure—and that is success. But what is the cure for success?
—DANIEL J. BOORSTIN

Well, most of us would probably say the answer is "more success." And that is the way most of us behave. Whether you're a movie star or an advertising executive, proverbial wisdom has it that you're only as good as your last picture or your last slogan. The question is not how good is he but how good can he get? No one rests on laurels anymore. This isn't ancient Rome, and the only way to come out a winner is to keep on running even when the race is over.

Right? Well, no, I don't think so. The question is, how much is enough? How many times do you need to do the high wire act before people down below really believe you can do it? You need to feel good about what you do, but self-worth isn't measured by external approval. If you tell that to yourself every day you just may start to believe it. The thing is, if you drive yourself right down to the corner of Addiction and Success, you just may never return.

A little success should go a long way. I'm going to allow myself to feel great about each success as it comes along and not just keep my eye on the bigger picture.

The art of being wise is the art of knowing what to overlook.   —WILLIAM JAMES

Men who do too much rarely, if ever, overlook anything. We always have a heightened sense of awareness, hypervigilant, always at the ready to take something, anything, on. Keeping things simple, streamlining our lives, does not come easy to us.

We're bloodhounds on the trail of a thousand kinds of game, picking up one scent after another, but rarely tracking down the prize.

We clutter our lives with our calendars, overlook an emotional ledger, until we no longer have a grip on anything. Wisdom comes when we learn to focus, and allow the extraneous to dissipate and disappear.

.~.

Today I'll make a note of the five most important tasks to complete—not six, not seven, just five. And tomorrow, I'll do it again.

Life is just one damned thing after another.
—ELBERT HUBBARD

Most of us gentlemen who overcommit are men who don't have a lot of fun. We don't play very much or very often. Laughter is a fairly foreign language. We don't engage easily in what some call "small talk." Oh, we have our golf outings, our tennis game. But more often than not it's all part of the day's work. Lunch with clients. Drinks with potential business partners. Golf with the boss. Days turn into nights, and life is mostly just one damned thing after another.

Is too much work and not enough play making us dull boys, as the saying goes? Worse, are we making those who love us unhappy, as they wait on the sidelines for the fun we once promised them to begin?

⌒

Today I'll plan to take some time to browse in a bookstore or read *Sports Illustrated,* rent a movie or take a walk, but I will not give up 100 percent of my day to work.

The necessities were going by default to save the luxuries until we hardly knew which were necessities and which were luxuries. —FRANK LLOYD WRIGHT

OK. Of course we know what the essentials are— we know the necessities of life include the roof over our heads, the groceries, the car payments, the heat, the electricity, the phone, the church, the insurance, the vacations, the extra TV, the VCR, the time-share in Aspen, the housekeeper, the gardener, the club dues, the season tickets to the ball games, the first class travel, the nanny, the "fun car," the IRS, the stockbroker, the lawyer, the accountant, well, you know . . .

More. More. More. Now all I need is an executive assistant to oversee my kingdom. Today I'll think about scaling back, downsizing, and how happy I was before I had so many things to watch over.

The more I want to get something done, the less I call it work. —RICHARD BACH

Work doesn't have to be a ball and chain. Work can be, and often is, quite fulfilling. When work begins to enslave us, we know it. We're overtired. Short-tempered. Prickly.

Motivation and work should go hand in hand. The more we take on, the more frustrated we become. If we're passionate about our work—or, to be less dramatic, we enjoy what we do—we do not call it work.

·∾·

I need to keep my mind open to what motivates me to work, and examine what that work is. There is nothing more taxing than facing a task that holds no mystery, no fascination, no passion.

FEBRUARY 1

*I think it pisses God off if you walk by the color purple
in a field somewhere and don't notice it.*
—ALICE WALKER

Maybe Alice Walker's famous words say, in part,
"Stop to smell the roses," but I think they also say
much more. I think these words tell us we're not on
earth just to push the boulder ahead of us; we're here
for a variety of reasons, but surely, we're here to
truly admire what has been put before us.

Those of us who would be hard-pressed to describe the layout of their own home need to heed Ms.
Walker's advice. We're running through the fields of
life at full tilt, and rarely, if ever, do we look from
side to side long enough to notice the color purple.

Let me be inspired today to look both ways before
I cross the street. Let me hope to stop and admire
the color purple.

I must keep aiming higher and higher—even though I know how silly it is. —ARISTOTLE ONASSIS

Interesting words from one of the most fabulously wealthy men in the world. When is enough enough? How much money is enough? How many trophies can we fit on the mantel? When does wealth equal happiness? Even Onassis knew it was silly, this never-ending grab for more.

When I was a young man, maybe just out of college, I thought that I'd probably top out in terms of income at about thirty-five thousand to forty thousand dollars per year, and wouldn't that be just right?

The drastic change in economy notwithstanding, I've changed my expectations over and over again. I've reached for more and more. It's time to think about the wealth of ideas and inner peace.

．～．

Today I'll not be so eager to think about my tangible wealth. Instead, I'll spend some time reflecting on the great riches my family and friends bestow upon me.

Live all you can; it's a mistake not to. It doesn't so much matter what you do in particular, so long as you have your life. If you haven't had that, what have you had?
—HENRY JAMES

Men who do too much would claim that we do have our lives. The trouble is, we have ours, and we're in charge of theirs, too.

Living all you can doesn't mean taking on everything in sight. It means, at least to me, that we need to live our moments to the fullest, without distraction, without duplicity of thought or action. James's quote also speaks implicitly of living one's own life by one's own definitions with inner directness. And it doesn't matter what you do, as long as you take pleasure in it, and the tasks inherent in your work don't own you.

.~.

Today I'm going to use the entire keyboard on the piano. But I'm going to play one of my favorite pieces of music.

Now that I'm here, where am I?   —JANIS JOPLIN

> At the Top of his Class
> Senior Vice President
> School Principal
> Head Foreman
> Chief Executive Officer
> Executive Chef
> Manager, Parts Department

Titles, classifications, identities, business cards. We're all consumed by them because they help define us. But men who do too much allow their business cards to define them entirely.

I was recently at a neighborhood gathering, and within twenty minutes every man had exchanged job information: "So, Bob, what do you do?" Does this make us feel safe? Are we hiding behind our "image" so that we can impress the world? The world has created us so it can sit back and judge us, too. Are we just going to sit back and let that happen? Or will we scratch beneath the surface in our conversations, get to know the man behind the business card?

When we're happy to exchange business cards, talk "shop," we're letting the other guy know where we are, not who we are.

～

I will try to exchange information with other men that exposes who I am, rather than who I want them to think I am.

I shall enjoy my freedom from the tyranny of the In and Out boxes.
   —S. DILLON RIPLEY, ON HIS RETIREMENT

For so many years I let the In and Out boxes dictate my days. Of course, I mean that figuratively, but nonetheless, like most of us men who do too much, I was in the position of putting out fires all day long. And that's when we know our lives are unmanageable (and the irony is, many of us are in charge of managing others).

I do not charge Mr. Ripley with workaholism, but his quote rings true for so many of us. Slaves to what others want, demand, or need, we do not examine what is in our In Boxes.

I do not want to retire to feel Mr. Ripley's sense of freedom. I want to incorporate my freedom into my work.

 ·~·

When you think about it, so much of what we think we must do every day is superfluous to our real jobs. Today I'm going to be very conscious of what is in my In Box. Most of it, no doubt, should have been placed in the Out Box.

Happiness may well consist primarily of an attitude toward time.   —ROBERT GRUDIN

The clock. Its face is often much angrier, much less forgiving than the faces of our superiors, our bosses, our supervisors.

Why are we tyrannized by the clock? Because men who do too much are trapped by time. We're slaves to the big and little hands. We work through lunch and are proud of it. We come home late from work too tired, too drained to enjoy our children or our wives or our partners. And we're proud of that, too.

Time is an enemy. And focusing on the fact that we all would like a thirty-six-hour day will only make us want a forty-two-hour day. We'll fill up the calendar, no matter how much time we're given.

◦∼◦

Today I'm going to attempt to go through the day without wearing my watch and without looking at the clock. If this little exercise makes me less aware of the time, and helps me to be more composed and less frantic, I may only wear my watch when it's absolutely necessary!

Life is God's novel. Let him write it.
  —ISAAC BASHEVIS SINGER

Men who do too much have much in common, but one of our major commonalities is our inability to "let go." We dream that we control our lives, and while we're awake we're certain of it.

If, as some assert, control is a myth, then that should give many of us cause for celebration. That doesn't mean we can't create our destiny, but we do need to loosen the reins a bit, let the plot unfold.

Think for a moment of the intricacy of each day of your life. There is so much more that goes into our lives than the events we control. Our efforts to control and write the shooting script for our lives shouldn't be abandoned. But we do need to allow our sense of control to free us; to feel a sense of uncertainty and revel in it.

◦∼◦

Today I will try to let the hours unfold. I'll throw away whatever script I had filed away and enjoy the uncertainty, the randomness of an unplanned, unscheduled twenty-four hours.

*Men who are unhappy, like men who sleep badly, are
always proud of the fact.* —BERTRAND RUSSELL

There is nobility in suffering. At least that's what
we've been taught all our lives. And there is a certain
pride we feel when we who are already proud to be
overtaxed announce that we've had little, if any, rest
the prior night.

The psychological treadmill, the one with no "off
button," is the vehicle of choice for those of us who
do too much.

We need to jump off the treadmill, take note of
our attitudes regarding our work and our unhappiness, and attempt to learn who our teacher was, and
why we need to relearn what he taught us.

~·

I need to take a hard look at my mentors and discover, if I can, if they were delighted with their
overcommitted lives and joyless at the same time.

Holding hands at midnight
'neath a starry sky,
Nice work if you can get it,
And you can get it if you try.
  —MUSIC BY GEORGE GERSHWIN
  —LYRICS BY IRA GERSHWIN

This popular tune was written during the Depression. And as wonderful as the melody and the lyrics are, it's a telling tune.

Romance was proclaimed dead around 1965, I think. Several attempts to revive it have failed. Romance can lie, it can hide truth, and it can create false, hurtful images.

But romance, in its purest, most unadulterated form, is at least diversionary, and at best, an expression of love and tenderness.

Men who do too much are too busy for romance. For the moment. For *a* moment. We're simply too tied up with our work to stop and hold hands beneath a starry sky.

Nice work if you can get it, and you can get it if you try.

～

I'll try to see my partner in a light today that makes us both look and feel better. And if I don't have someone in my life right now, I'll think about how I can incorporate a person into my life, and value her or him in all the right ways.

A great many people have come up to me and asked how I manage to get so much work done and still keep looking so dissipated. —ROBERT BENCHLEY

No secret here. Not really. Looking haggard is our badge of honor.

I've often thought one of the most brazen acts of self-indulgence was to see a couple of the guys from the office go to the gym at lunchtime, play some handball, or a pickup game of basketball, or take a swim. How self-involved can you get!

No, now I know it's those of us who knock back a bad sandwich while working like crazy, right through lunch, who are self-indulgent.

·~·

Taking time for oneself always looks suspect, especially if you're a man who does too much. Today I'll knock off early. Take a walk, swim, or read the entire newspaper. Maybe I'll incorporate that hour into each day.

Look at me. Worked myself up from nothing to a state of extreme poverty. —S. J. PERELMAN

Always a favorite of mine, and millions of other readers of first-rate satire, Perelman was a shrewd observer.

The irony, of course, is that when one of our accounts is healthy and the envy of many, our personal ledger is grossly out of line. Some of the richest men I know are some of the craziest. Many of them are so obsessed with their net worth that they barely know the ages of their children, let alone how to take time for themselves, learn a new talent, or indulge in a fantasy just for the sake of having fun.

There's a whole range of bankruptcies. So many have nothing to do with money.

～

Today I'll do my best to examine the ratio of work to pleasure. Is there a balance?

God is not dead, but alive and well and working on a much less ambitious project.
—ANONYMOUS GRAFFITI

Is society in trouble? Some of the change we see around us is healthy. But there are many who believe we've really lost track of our basic goals; we've filled our days with compulsive behaviors and have stopped learning how to trust our fundamental selves.

Life is an ambitious project. We need to learn that it is as simple or as complicated as we want to make it.

∙∽∙

I want to be clear in what I want, and where it will lead me. I'll think about my father or mother, the arc of their lives, and their ambitions for guidance and reflection.

A bayonet is a weapon with a worker at each end.
—ANONYMOUS

If I don't kill you, you'll kill me. Right? So much of our work is combative. If we reduced negotiation scenarios to this image, it might be more accurate than we'd like to imagine.

Men who do too much travel in packs. We surround ourselves with the great overcommitted. And the pack mentality always gets out of hand.

Verbal bayonets are everywhere. In the workplace, they are unsheathed at the drop of a hat. The irony is, of course, that there are rarely any real winners at the end of a violent confrontation. The man left standing often dies days after the competition.

·~·

Tug of war is not a game I want to play. But it is a game familiar to men who do too much. I will try hard not to be combative in my interactions at work and at home.

One of the symptoms of the approaching nervous breakdown is the belief that one's work is terribly important, and that to take a holiday would bring all kinds of disaster. —BERTRAND RUSSELL

Remember, that is not the only sign of an impending nervous breakdown, but it's a major tipoff.

How many vacations have been interrupted by the "emergency" phone call? How many times have we had a day of rest turned into a day of anguish because we assumed the worst? Something, anything, was going terribly wrong back at the office.

How can the shop possibly operate without me? Very well, most of the time. Sometimes better because I'm away, I've found out. Especially when I'm stressed out. When my behavior is frenetic, I keep co-workers off-balance, and productivity drops.

Bertrand Russell is right.

.~.

As soon as I begin to feel that tragedy is looming due to my impending absence, I will examine my feelings and, as best I can, take the long view of work, and understand that the roof will not cave in simply because I'm not there for it to hit me.

There is nothing more tragic than to find an individual bogged down in the length of life devoid of breadth.
—MARTIN LUTHER KING, JR.

Most of us are very good at measuring things: How fast? How far? How long?

Yes, we all think about our longevity—how many years have we left on earth? But not many of us are asking, What will I do with the days I have remaining? Not just filling the hours, but with what? Will I begin a new career? Raise a first or second family? Will I fall in love again? What will I lose, and what will I gain?

Quality of life is an overworked phrase, but in reality it is underused, and rarely ever applied to our daily lives. How do we begin to think about tomorrow?

～

My newly found idle moments give me a great amount of inner peace. I value those moments and will make time for more of them. This is how I will begin to discover the breadth of my life, the past, and the future.

What you have become is the price you paid to get what you used to want.   —MIGNON MCLAUGHLIN

Not a pretty picture. Driven. And now, most of us know that what we wanted yesterday, what we nearly broke our necks and those necks around us for, really wasn't worth it.

There is an inherent tragedy in being obsessed with wanting. The tragedy lies in how we go about getting what we want, but moreover, it gives us the double whammy of finding out that we don't really want what we asked for.

·~·

I must caution myself when I begin to lust after something. Is my hunger for it going to supplant my values, or will my failure to get it take a greater toll? It's once again time to stop, and to think.

For him who has no concentration, there is no tranquility.
—BHAGAVAD GITA

This idea of true concentration, of course, is foreign to most of us men who do too much. After all, how can you concentrate, deeply focus yourself, when you're answering the telephone, opening the mail, and writing a business letter simultaneously (all the time watching the clock because you're late for an appointment)?

There is no tranquility because we've never learned to value quietness. For us, the evidence of success is a Materhorn of paper on our desks, of ringing telephones and buzzing fax machines.

Only recently has daydreaming come into its own; some men now understand why looking out the window opens the mind.

⌁

I will try to take a few moments out of every hour to look into space, clear my head and allow myself to listen to my breathing—the pause that refreshes.

What we love to do we find time to do.
—JOHN LANCASTER SPALDING

Many of us are so busy accomplishing something to help keep us from finding out what it is we might like, or even love to do, that by the end of the day all we can do is something mediocre, something that gives us little if any pleasure.

I know a number of men who have never asked themselves what they love to do. I don't mean watching a good football game or eating pizza and having a beer. I mean what are they passionate about? What would they really ache to do?

OK, maybe golf, or chess, or tennis, but I'm talking about really addressing yourself, going deeper, and coming up with the kind of unadulterated passion we had as kids. Go back to it, at least for a visit in your head. It will be rejuvenating and invigorating.

⁓

Men who do too much have no time to do what they love. I will make a real committed effort to take one day a week and discover what it is that gives me satisfaction, peace, and passion.

I'll be damned if I'll be a public utility.
  —HENRY R. LUCE

We're all so afraid of failure, especially if our short-comings should be in any way public.

That's why we need to seek moderation in so many of the things we do. If we're committed to rediscovering what is important to us, we will re-create a system by which we can live, and not live out our days as a public or private utility.

～

Men who do too much are, to a great degree, shame-based. I need to be aware that my failures teach me as much as my successes, and that obsession with work masks my pain.

The glow of one warm thought is to me worth more than money. —THOMAS JEFFERSON

Ideas. Thoughts. Inventions. Introspection. Memories of joyful days or nights. These are things that most of us never pause to make time for.

The lust and need for money is sometimes the culprit. But when we are really deep in our disease, we do not even need the cash carrot—we'll overwork on command.

Most men define themselves not by who they are but by what they have. Money. Cars. Trophy wives and girlfriends. Position. Power.

.∼.

I will give myself permission to have warm thoughts today. I will allow myself the time to revel in a memory or in a fantasy. Enjoy it. Let the glow stay with me.

Personal relations are the important things for ever and ever, and not the outer life of telegrams and anger.
  —E. M. FORSTER

Friendship. Now there's an alien concept for men who do too much. Our overcommitment gives us reason not to cultivate friendships. And friendships don't just spring up like dandelions in April.

Friendships take time. They must be tended. Nurtured. But the joy that is inherent in a trusting, long-term friendship is nearly impossible to describe. But not impossible to engender.

.~.

I know it is important to have friends. I am not whole without someone I can trust and who can trust me. I will begin to look at those I know with an eye toward developing friendships.

A salesman is got to dream, boy. It comes with the territory. —ARTHUR MILLER

Dreaming is so important, so life affirming, so self-nurturing. If we deny that we need to dream, then we lose all hope. The light goes out. Even Willie Loman knew that.

In our own worlds, no matter what or where they are, we need to allow ourselves hope. It is ennobling. It makes us better, kinder, more open people.

Dreams don't come easily to men who do too much. We've grown up and think we haven't time for them. But it's dreams that keep us alive.

.~.

Looking up into the sky brings on dreams. I think I'll spend some time looking at the tops of trees today.

Never confuse motion with action.
  —ERNEST HEMINGWAY

Many of us, ever since we were little boys in grade school, learned or knew innately how to "look busy." Later, when the situation called for it, and it often did, we'd look exceptionally busy.

This busyness kept at bay any intimacy, any commitment, any real and positive steps toward our inner well-being or peace.

We learned that motion is honorable, even if it's primarily camouflage.

Action implies decision, accomplishment, commitment. Action is not motion. We do get the two concepts confused.

~

I'm not going to behave frantically in order to mask my emotions, or merely to "look busy." I'm going to learn the difference between motion and action.

Every Man is entitled to be valued by his best moments.
—RALPH WALDO EMERSON

Too often we reflect on those times that we didn't "perform," didn't live up to someone else's expectations. And others often judge us when we're at our worst. Rarely do men judge other men by recalling their finest moments.

Even sports stars, men who have perfected a fastball or a jump shot, or skated a perfect 10, are now scrutinized unmercifully by the press, and like lemmings, many of us are falling right in line and criticizing these great athletes on the basis of their last failure rather than their last success.

～•

It will elevate me and my peers to begin viewing other men in their best light, at their best moments.

Loafing needs no explanation and is its own excuse.
   —CHRISTOPHER MORLEY

The word *loaf* is like a four-letter curse word to the overextended. It's unthinkable to loaf. Loafing is a sign of laziness. Loafing brings on self-criticism and self-loathing.

   But loafing is recharging. I love a rainy Saturday when I can stay at home, not get dressed, and not feel that I have to feel bad about it. I don't feel I've failed if I kick off for the day and vegetate. It's healthy.

•~•

I will choose a day or two each month to disappear, hang around the house, and just goof off. I won't paint the garage or clean out the attic. I'll do as little as I can.

The secret of success is consistency of purpose.
—BENJAMIN DISRAELI

Those of us who are neck-deep in commitment are drowning in a brew composed from a reckless recipe.

One of the ways we become mired in obsessive work is to lose track of purpose. We become dissuaded and march to new, if not different, drummers, change courses in the middle of the race, and mix metaphors until we're awash in a stew that stagnates and renders us incapable of promises.

That is our only consistency.

~

Today I will focus on purpose. That's what I need to do. I will not sink into the abyss that leaves me no choice.

*Our dignity is not in what we do, but what we
understand.* —GEORGE SANTAYANA

Men need tangible proof of what they're worth. But
ideas, despite their immense importance, are not tangible. Moreover, men who do too much are generally
too preoccupied with performance to value "ideas."
This limits their choices and mutes their courage to
explore and create.

Finally, it undermines their emotional well-being
and erodes their dignity.

·~·

In pacing myself today, I will think about what I
understand, not just what I produce.

It is an old ironic habit of human beings to run faster when we have lost our way. —ROLLO MAY

How true. Famous psychotherapist Rollo May's words are so telling. Men who do too much know little about moderation. We tend to turn up the heat without regard to the problems at hand; motion camouflages indecision or lack of focus.

We need to teach ourselves that our failure to always be on course is part of life's process. We need to be kinder to ourselves and for the sake of our health and for those who care for us, SLOW DOWN.

⟂

When I catch myself behaving frantically, I'll stop and think about my reason for it, and attempt to focus on the task at hand.

FEBRUARY 29

The passion for order can poison the soul.
—ANONYMOUS

Contrary to popular belief, one can be overboard when it comes to organization. When men who do too much are seized by order it often signals their denial of a range of emotional issues. It can mean that there is an unwillingness to confront sorrow, grief, love, or emotional commitment.

When we're overordered we kill spontaneity and inhibit free thought and dreams. If there is a place for everything, does it really mean everything needs to be in its place?

～

I will be mindful of my need to categorize, organize, overdefine. I will try to be freer in my thoughts and my actions.

To be idle requires a strong sense of personal identity.
—ROBERT LOUIS STEVENSON

I find myself pacing the room as I talk on the phone. I like to have the television news on while I read one of the four newspapers I receive every day. I need to have music on in the background at the office. I tell people it helps calm me.

I'm often up out of my seat at dinner, sometimes clearing the table before everyone is finished eating. All of this sounds kind of funny until I reflect on it and realize that each of these traits is a manifestation of a man who does too much.

.~.

I was taught that to be idle was to be lazy. I need to learn to sit still, be still, and allow myself some time for introspection.

The day is of infinite length for him who knows how to appreciate and use it. —GOETHE

How many times have we said, "I need another three or four hours every day to get my work done?"

I'm coming to understand that it wouldn't matter if I had twenty-six-hour days. I'd still have too much work on my desk.

There are, of course, practical approaches to inhibiting our need for more time. Taking less on is one way I've begun to deal with my tendency to overcommit. That may be a luxury in some ways, but scaling back our expectations of our selves is part of the equation, too. I know I'm incapable of certain kinds of work as well as a massive work load.

Do I want to be rich and die young, or have somewhat less, materially, and be around long enough to appreciate my old age?

~·

Learning how to apportion time and tasks is a lifelong process. I'll try to focus on my strengths today, or not take on too much.

A man is rich in proportion to the number of things he can afford to leave alone.
—HENRY DAVID THOREAU

Simplify, simplify, simplify. I believe that word, and that philosophy will be important as we move through the nineties and into the next century. I think all of us men who do too much need to scale back in virtually every conceivable way.

We're overburdened by choice, of course. The eighties helped us behave like overcommitted zealots and now we must take the time to let go of the extraneous.

Men who do too much are always looking for diversions. Let us now turn our attention to simplification. It will be liberating.

·~·

I will try to have the courage to become rich by assuming less.

The real problem of your leisure is how to keep other people from using it. —ANONYMOUS

Leisure? What leisure?

Men who do too much always have trouble with boundaries. We go away on vacations, looking forward to some R&R, promising our wives, families, and friends that *we will not go near a telephone.*

We really do not understand the conflict we have with work. We need to see that we have choices, and that we can set boundaries between work and play.

It is difficult, as the above quote states, especially for men who do too much, to say: "No, I'm not available to you today, or tomorrow, or on the weekend."

.~.

I need to be aware that it may be my leisure, and how I observe it, that helps keep my balance.

Each day, and the living of it, has to be a conscious creation in which discipline and order are relieved with some play and some pure foolishness.
—MAY SARTON

One of the most rejuvenating things I can do for myself is to let go and act silly with my children.

I will admit that I have a sense of well-being and some peace when I get a job done. But nothing relieves my stress like laughter, rolling around, and being crazy with people I care about.

.~.

I will try and make myself available for some pure foolishness every day.

MARCH 6

There is only one success—to be able to spend life in your own way. —CHRISTOPHER MORLEY

You can define your life pretty much the way you want to. Money doesn't do that for you. You have to learn to live with your feelings, appreciate your heart more than your head. Then you have a multitude of choices about how you live your life.

It is a myth that great fortunes set us free. It has been proven over and over that money makes us slaves to our wealth, keeps us hypervigilant, constantly fearful that we'll lose it all, wake up one day with an empty vault.

•~•

I do not think it's too late to direct the course of my life. I will take a hard look at some of the choices I've made, and then consider some change.

I think knowing what you can not do is more important than knowing what you can do. —LUCILLE BALL

Lucy was right. It is so fundamentally important to know what our strengths are and try to do less of what we're not good at that it seems all too simple.

But how many of us men who do too much are doing the wrong things too much? It is not just the volume of things that take up our days. It is the choice of tasks with which we've saddled ourselves.

We spend a great deal of time denying that we have weaknesses, or that we aren't good at everything. And that really makes us not very good at anything.

~

I need to take inventory of what I do and what I do not like to do, and decide if the second list is dangerously close to duplicating the first.

*We should all do what in the long run gives us joy, even
if it is only picking grapes or sorting the laundry.*
—E. B. WHITE

Most men's fantasies run along the same lines, I
think: Power, wealth, independence, peace. Now I
haven't done a scientific study about this, but I've
read a great deal and have talked to a lot of men
about the BIG issues.

I've talked with my wife about what our children
might grow up to "be." I've always said that if they're
truly happy pumping gas or picking grapes, that's fine
with me. The key here is happiness. Not what makes
me happy, or proud, or what looks good to their
peers. What I get joy from is very different than what
the next guy gets joy from.

.~.

My expectations for myself are just that. I will not
superimpose my expectations on others, certainly not
my children. I will think about the essence of what
gives *me* joy.

One machine can do the work of fifty ordinary men. No machine can do the work of one extraordinary man.
—ELBERT HUBBARD

This is the age of new technologies. From megabyte computers to magnetic resonance imaging, we are a people dazzled by the machines we've created. And while we should be in awe of what these new machines provide us, what about the soul of our own machine—our gifts, our intellects, our ability to interpret thoughts and emotions?

The minds of the men who helped create the "great machines" are the essence of what is truly great. And there is still no machine that can soothe a child's fears, feed hungry people, and give warmth to a cold, lost, angry heart. That is what makes us extraordinary. Every one of us.

Today I'll pause and think about my strengths; what's extraordinary about me.

If I would be a young man again and had to decide how to make my living, I would not try to become a scientist or scholar or teacher. I would rather choose to be a plumber or a peddler in the hope to find that modest degree of independence still available under present circumstances.   —ALBERT EINSTEIN

Even though written in 1954, Einstein's words are especially appropriate today. In the world we've created, where action is more likely to be rewarded than that which has been produced, we have lost a great deal of our independence. When our lives become unmanageable by virtue of our need to take too much on, we are reminded of a simpler, less complicated life that we might have lead.

In making our lives simpler, more focused, we set ourselves free, and give ourselves more than a mea-sure of independence.

∽·

I will do my best today to strive for independence. It will mean that I will need to lessen my load, by not taking on the world.

Beware the naked man who offers you his shirt.
—HARVEY MACKAY

This title of Mackay's book comes from an old African proverb, and it's a wise one, too. If we promise others the sun, the moon, the stars, and a twelve-hour workday, we are fooling everyone. In promising too much, we end up being unable to really give anything.

Often we are well intentioned, but cannot possibly deliver what we promise. It is unwise for us to offer too much and then, time after time, fail, not only those to whom we give our promise but finally failing ourselves. We hide behind our promises, thinking that what we give will make up for what we do not have.

～

Today I will not give so much of myself that I end up angry, disappointed, and a failure in every- or anyone else's eyes.

Whose life is it, anyway? ———BRIAN CLARK

When we're really at our workaholic worst, we forget we have any choices. We hide behind routine, we take perverse pride in the prisons we've created, but we claim that "life" has dealt us an unbearable, impossible hand.

Whose life, indeed? When we hide behind the mountains of tasks we have created, we say: "I'm not good enough," "I shouldn't enjoy life," "I cannot create a joyful, meaningful life."

·~·

Today I'll see my work load for what it is—a self-created monster that's made the word *choice* obsolete in my language. And I'll run the phrase *whose life is it, anyway?* through my head until I understand that it's mine.

Opera is when a guy gets stabbed in the back and, instead of bleeding, he sings. —ED GARDNER

Soap opera is when we've created a scenario that inevitably gets us stabbed in the back. We keep on moving, keep on singing, keep on working, never admitting we've been wounded. The opera goes on, as we sing and sing, work and work.

Workaholics rarely have the courage for self-confrontation. We're too busy trying to control, fearing that if we pause to examine our actions, we really will bleed—right to the last gasp.

❧

Today I'll think about what really makes me strong. Is it the self-perpetrating myth of my grandiosity, or can it be that acceptance and tolerance of my weaknesses will make me all the stronger?

*He (Harris) felt the loyalty we all feel to
unhappiness—the sense that that is where we really
belong.* —GRAHAM GREENE

Self-abuse comes in an endless variety of behavioral
forms. Workaholism is certainly a form of self-abuse,
and one that is particularly destructive to those we
love and those who love us.

And it's an endless cycle, once it starts. We abuse
others—our wives, children, friends—not knowing
it, we pull them in. Finally, we feel that we are
doomed. This is, we believe, our lot in life. We begin,
as Graham Green says, to feel loyal to our unhappiness, and the cycle of self-abuse continues.

～

I will try to become disloyal to my unhappiness; I
will dare to question my cycle of self-abuse and become aware of how my self-abuse has created its own
fortress of loneliness.

Vaster is man than his works.
—ROCKWELL KENT

We define ourselves and others as well by what "they do." In almost any social setting, where a group of men congregate, there is a moment where each man describes "what he does." This territorial definition serves a number of purposes, but more and more I see something in that exchange far more sinister than what appears on the surface.

In this setting men are proving to one another (and this extends to men relating to women as well), that they work the hardest, have the most responsibility, the most demanding careers, and finally, this exchange serves to define the individuals.

Our work is not us. We are so many things. We need not subject ourselves to the most common and misleading denomination: our work.

~·

Today I will try to define myself to others not in terms of my work, or a physical manifestation of my career, but rather another, deeper kind of self-disclosure.

Despair is the price one pays for setting oneself an impossible aim. —GRAHAM GREENE

Denial is at the very root of all addiction, work addiction included, since addicts can never get enough (or *give* enough), and this encourages despair. As Graham Greene says, it is inevitable that we should experience the dark depression because we've set ourselves up for it.

If we deny that we've set impossible goals, we will always be incomplete, disappointed with our performances.

.~.

Today and every day I will remind myself that high standards may be confused with impossibilities.

He that would govern others, first should be Master of himself. —PHILIP MASSINGER

Workaholics are perfectionists. Perfectionism is a disease in and of itself, but when you dictate perfectionism it can only lead to destruction.

Are you a supervisor at work? Do you have people reporting to you? Do they constantly fail you by not turning in perfect performances, perfect products, faultless reports?

Flexibility with oneself and with others leads to maximum effectiveness. If you're in the role of leader, then you must be tolerant of mistakes, of uneven performances, of demands not met. To be otherwise is to be a blatantly practicing workaholic.

～

The concept of perfection is a myth, and I will keep that in mind as I go through my day, interacting with those with whom I work.

When I grow up I want to be a little boy.
— JOSEPH HELLER

Since denial knows no age and we begin to use it as children, many of us men never have a chance to be children. If we've come from a dysfunctional family, we are robbed of our childhood. In order to survive as we grow up, we become consumed in proving our self-worth. Many of us do that by immersing ourselves in our work, making ourselves our work, designing ourselves based on our work.

The freedom "normal" children enjoy is anathema to us. We risk our very self-images if faced with that kind of freedom. That is why we run from it, and drown the work and commitment we've created for ourselves.

～

Today I'll take some time out to be a little boy. I'm going to trade some grown-up behavior for some freeing "play time."

You no longer spend your life hurrying around the corner for something which is never there.
—REX HARRISON

Obviously Harrison is talking about experience and growth, and the folly of youth. But I think there's more to it than that. So many of us run and run, always looking for *the* answer, *the* tonic, compulsively looking beyond what is in front of us.

Work junkies are marathon runners. The act of work intoxicates us, the act of work enhances our faulty self-image, and we're forever after that which is just around the corner, and the next corner, and the next.

.~.

Today I'm pacing out my day in a way in which I am not breathless, emotionless, and fearful. I will be mindful of whatever it is that is guiding my actions.

It is said to begin with the father.
—MAXINE KUMIN

Our fathers, in most cases, are our first models of behavior. We emulate their good qualities and copy their bad behavior.

I can think of no exception to this: Every man I know who is a workaholic and who will admit it also tells the sad tale of his father's workaholism. They tell stories of their fathers' inability to keep promises, their forgetfulness, their perfectionism. And, finally, their emotional absenteeism.

With us men especially, it does indeed begin with the father.

~

If I can force myself to remember my father at his work, I can force myself to understand him, and force myself not to repeat his performance.

The toughest thing about success is that you've got to keep on being a success. —IRVING BERLIN

What a nightmare success can spawn. Especially for those of us addicted to it. How can we top what we just did? Can I be manager of the year three years running? How can I be the top sales rep year after year? How can I drive any faster, any further? And who is judging my performances? My sales ratios?

We need to learn how to fail, when to fail, and what, if anything, it will cost us to fail. We need to constantly ask whom we are performing for and what got us on this success treadmill in the first place.

.~.

I want to look to my little successes—things that give me momentary happiness and a sense of well-being. I want to be less inclined to look to the grand successes and not get caught up with them.

Nothing is more terrible than ignorance in action.
　—GOETHE

Compulsion is a manifestation of addiction. So many of us, whether in business or within the family, are constantly active. Workaholics are activity junkies. We get involved in change for the sake of change; newness carries authority, and we're rarely informed enough to make decisions based on information. It takes too much time. It holds us back. It slows things down. The more ignorant we are, the more decisive we can be. We workaholics find a pace slower than ours to be suspect.

．～．

The more I'm examining all the traits of doing too much, the more I'm discovering those behaviors that cover for my addiction. Today I'll make a very conscious effort to slow down and uncomplicate the workplace of which I'm a part.

What shall the world do with its children?
There are lives the executives
know nothing of . . .
The other world is like a thorn
In the ear of a tiny beast.
   —ROBERT BLY

When I reflect on all the years I worked in New York in major corporations, I remember the inhumanity of the workplace. The environment of most organizations is a hotbed of institutionalized workaholism. As in a beehive, there are breeders and there are soldiers; there is a massive and fairly sophisticated caste system, but each level supports the next, and it's an ugly, dehumanizing place to be.

Those who have power in the workplace want to know nothing of family. The addict fits in here well, because he wants to serve the powerful, and the family be damned.

·~·

I want to incorporate my work life more with my personal life. I see myself in a more holistic way now, less compartmentalized, and I want my workplace to be a humane place to be.

I don't like work—no man does—but I like what is in work—the chance to find yourself. Your own reality—for yourself, not for others—what no other man can ever know. —JOSEPH CONRAD

Working at something you love, something you're passionate about, is almost always rewarding.

When I'm at my healthiest, I can immerse myself in my work. I go deep into it and find peace there. When I am at my best, I give something pure of myself. I don't feel driven. I don't feel coerced. I don't feel the need to escape, either. I'm truly at peace.

·~·

If I have the luxury of it, the space for it, I need to attempt to isolate the part of my work that I really enjoy. Not for the sense of escape, but for "that chance to find myself."

Some men are born mediocre, some men achieve mediocrity, and some men have mediocrity thrust upon them. —JOSEPH HELLER

We are not all equal. I have some talents that the next man does not, and the reverse, of course, is true.

What we need to stop believing is that we must excel at everything we take on. I know a number of men—any one of them could be elected to the Workaholics Hall of Fame—who are absolutely driven to perfect everything they undertake. If it's downhill skiing, then they must hit the top slopes at Aspen. If it's scuba diving, they turn what might be fun into some twisted need to see how deep and for how long they can stay submerged. And if it's work related—well, you know the rest.

And paradoxically, that's when they're at their most mediocre. In pushing themselves to every conceivable limit, they've diluted themselves in other ways. The families of these men are lonely. And the men themselves are, too.

⋅∼⋅

The idea is to enjoy life. Soak it in, feel it, and have some fun with it. I know what I'm good at and what I'm not good at. Pushing myself beyond my borders is compulsive and destructive, and I'm going to try not to do it.

There are no second acts in American lives.
  —F. SCOTT FITZGERALD

No second acts anywhere, as far as I know.

But those of us given to excess somehow believe that we'll have time for the kids next Wednesday, or that we'll cancel the trip this year, but that will give us more time to plan it for next year. Or the dentist appointment will just have to wait, I've got a big fish on the end of my line at the office.

We really do believe, even if we don't put words to it, that we have more time, or at least "another time."

I'm horrified at how quickly my kids are growing and how few years I have left with my parents. I'm equally appalled by my delusions about time in general. And I share this dual time zone with all my peers who do too much.

.~.

I am making a concerted effort not to let time get away from me. It's too valuable to spend on work all day and into the evening.

So now he is a legend when he would have preferred to be a man. —JACQUELINE KENNEDY ONASSIS

"Be careful," we're told, "of what we ask for, because we might get it."

When we take on too much, it takes its toll on us, and on those we love and those who love us. When all we ever wanted hasn't proven to be enough, we're in big trouble.

But grandiosity is so seductive. And "greatness" may be too high a goal. "Fulfillment" might be a better one. Or perhaps we should aspire to become, as Ms. Onassis says, "a man."

·~·

There is no one who does not have his share of inconsistencies, of mixed emotions and dueling ideologies. But I will try to be clear about who I am and how I want others to see me.

It's not the men in my life that counts—it's the life in my men. —MAE WEST

I don't think Mae West would, in this day, claim to be a practitioner of polymonogamy. (I think that term was made up between Phil Donahue and Oprah Winfrey.)

But dear old Mae had a point. "Quality of quantity" might have been a more genteel way of putting it. But the more we take on, the thinner we spread ourselves, the less we have to offer. Quality diminishes.

Mae West would have seen through any of us workaholics. She probably would have said: "Men who do too much will never do too much for me."

～

Sometimes we need to laugh at ourselves, our predicaments, our obsessions. This is a day to do that. Today I'll have a good laugh at my own expense.

Hear that lonesome whipporwill?
He sounds too blue to fly.
The midnight train is whining low,
I'm so lonesome I could cry.
—HANK WILLIAMS

Music often creates a feeling that gives us the impetus to talk, even to ourselves, ruminating about past sadnesses, current tragedies, or great moments in memory.

But what I think about when I hear these words by Hank Williams is desperation, and how we cover that feeling up with denial, our work, and our perfectionism.

Williams is crying out loud—something a workaholic never does. He's saying he's hurting, he's lonesome, and he needs someone. Men who do too much don't need *anyone,* they need *everyone.* Williams isn't denying his loneliness; he's awash in it, and sings about it.

⌣

If I feel lonely today, or particularly sad about someone or something, I'm going to give in to it, not deny it; I'm going to let myself *feel* it.

Doubt grows with knowledge.   —GOETHE

The older I get, the more questions I ask. I know less, I'm certain of fewer things and ideas; I'm less dogmatic. I'm more open.

Overextending myself used to cover up all of my doubts. After all, when you're extremely busy, who has time to contemplate anything? And I've been so busy I've become forgetful. My memory is as short as my attention span.

Busyness covers a multitude of inequities, frustrations, sadness, doubts. When I'm more measured in my thoughts and activities, I make time for my doubts.

∙～∙

The more I know, the less I'm certain. I will be mindful of being open to my doubts today, and in future days.

The intellect of man is forced to choose perfection of the life, or of the work. And if it takes the second, it must refuse a heavenly mansion, raging in the dark.
—WILLIAM BUTLER YEATS

Yeats was truly brilliant, and perhaps in his day he felt that there were two diverging paths, and only two. But I believe, even though it is difficult and demanding, we can have a bit of both.

Do we need to excel in all phases of our work? Or do we need to plunge headlong and forever into our spiritually and intellectually rich inner life, at the expense of our "work" or career?

I suppose we *feel* we must choose between the two. We're told we must choose. A spiritual leader, whether he be a priest, a shaman, or a medicine man, is not a man who also has work or a career. Historically, we have no models for a hybrid life. But we need to interweave these two components of life lest we miss the heavenly mansion raging in the dark.

～・

Choosing perfection on either path is dangerous. I hope to be able to create a life that takes both the spiritual and the less lofty, but often rewarding work, and create a balance.

The danger of the past was that men became slaves. The danger of the future is that men may become robots.
—ERICH FROMM

Slaves are robots and vice versa. When we allow others to have power over us to the extent that we lose ourselves, our values, our choices, we become slaves. When we do that to ourselves, we become victims of addiction. We degrade ourselves and those who care for us when our self-expectation borders on the absurd.

When we are rational and caring for ourselves, we do not let the slave/robot system take over. We are mindful and respectful of ourselves.

ॱᐁॱ

The concept of robotics is a machinist's and work-aholic's dream come true. I'm not on anybody's assembly line, and I'll pace myself according to my needs, not anyone else's.

My candle burns at both ends;
It will not last the night;
But, ah, my foes, and, oh, my friends—
It gives a lovely light.
  —EDNA ST. VINCENT MILLAY

Yes, that is a memorable light, but a short-lived glow.

Some of us would burn the candle at the middle, too, if there were a way. We exhaust ourselves, use ourselves up, and all of our energy disappears when we take on too much.

Our shelf life diminishes. We get old before our time. We do not know how to pace ourselves, how to measure out our time. When we are young, our ignorance is the reason for the exuberance. But at some point, we need to see that the lovely light Edna St. Vincent Millay referred to is not the light to live by but the heat that burns.

~

I need to know my limitations, how much I can afford to give. Today I'll measure my energy and be prudent in what I promise.

If Dad's first love was his work, we take our job to be
our full-time mistress and wonder if Dad is watching from
his grave as we work ourselves into an early one.
—JOHN LEE

It is a fact that many of us, unknowingly and unwittingly, act out precisely what we perceived our father's role in life was.

We can talk on and on about not committing the same mistakes, recreating the same terms and horrors that our fathers visited upon us, but our lack of a clear view and our ever-present system of denial often makes us perfect mimics of the behavior we abhor.

Our sense of what is appropriate is first dictated by our fathers, and if we are not questioning students, we mime the same destructive behaviors.

⌇

I will question my father's work patterns, whether well intentioned or not, and ask myself if I'm walking in his footsteps.

We are confronted with insurmountable opportunities.
　—POGO

We all know people (if this doesn't describe us) who, when presented with a multipage menu in a restaurant, have an almost impossible time making a decision about what to order.

Men who do too much see a menu like that every day. We tend to see opportunities everywhere. We want to hit all the bases, and in so doing, we rarely hit any of them.

When we're confronted by choices, we can't make one. We make four or five or twelve. In our disease we are indeed confronted by choice. We want and need it all.

～

I endanger my well-being when I am unfocused. When there exists a plethora of possibilities I overindulge. Today I'll prioritize my opportunities and tackle only the most important ones, and do the same tomorrow.

Martyrdom . . . is the only way in which a man can become famous without ability.
   —GEORGE BERNARD SHAW

Many of us are martyrs. And it doesn't really mean we haven't any abilities, but it does mean that we are more attuned to doing too much than to doing what we're best suited to do. We clutter our lives with "duties," translate our work into "favors," and set up a massive house of cards the foundation of which is composed of denial.

Martyrs are unhappy. They are not really giving of themselves. They are not, in any way, balanced. And martyrs do not question these motivations but are men who can come to only one conclusion: I am doing too much, but I am doing it for *you.*

.~.

I am not interested in becoming famous for my martyrdom, but I am interested in discovering why I need to feel like a martyr.

Who loves ya, baby?
  —TELLY SAVALAS AS *Kojak*

One of the reasons we overextend ourselves is that we really don't think anyone loves us. We aren't good enough to get the love we need unless we prove it through our work.

Our answer then is, "Nobody loves me, baby." So low is our self-esteem, our inability to take time for ourselves and to see ourselves as "lovable" people, that we cover up our true feelings with work and more work.

The concept of love is, indeed, a kind of work in itself!

∙∿∙

I need to allow people to love me because I have value, I am a kind and giving person and I am every bit as worthy as the next guy.

Three o'clock is always too late or too early for anything you want to do. —JEAN-PAUL SARTRE

We worker bees are so rigid, so time oriented, so task directed that even though we may be disorganized, we still have a set time of the day that we adhere to. While it may seem contradictory, the man who does too much has his own clock and his own calendar, and the world had better observe them.

Three o'clock is a funny time. Some of us workaholics think that it's too late to start a new task, or too early to begin winding down. We see all our work as mountains; there is very little differential in the size of any job. It's all daunting and distressing. And there's never a good time to begin or end any of them.

～

Structure may be seen as a bandage, for some of us, but if it helps just a little, we need to apportion our time to fit the task, not to see everything before us on the same scale.

In a dream you are never eighty.
  —ANNE SEXTON

Many of us are dreaming whether asleep or awake. We have an idea of who we are, of what our work is, and yes, of how old we are.

Scientists say that we perceive ourselves as between ten and fifteen years younger than we are.

Denial of our real age is common for workaholics. We're always playing catch-up! "How is it possible I'm almost thirty-nine?" "Where did the last six months go?" We're never in the present; we're either in the future, dreaming about how it will be when we have some free time and all our work is done, or thinking about the past and lamenting how we misappropriated our time.

~·

Workaholics don't operate in the here and now— more often in the past and future. I will be mindful of the moment, and not obsessed with "what's next."

*The length of a meeting rises with the square of the
number of people present.*
    —ATTRIBUTED TO EILEEN SHANAHAN

Most of us in a business setting or who belong to any
organization where meetings take place, understand
Eileen Shanahan's quote.

Especially when a group of men who do too much
gets together, you can sure bet that any meeting will
be endless. We all want to be heard, we all want to
lead, and we all want to make the decisions. And we
are the best at dissecting an issue until it is no longer
recognizable.

It's not just the length of the meeting, either. It's
how many we feel we must have. We're happiest, of
course, when our calendars are stuffed to overflowing
with appointments and meetings.

If I'm in a situation where I can make a decision
without calling a meeting, I will make a conscious
effort to do so; not to undermine the group but, in
fact, for the good of the group.

It is easy ... terribly easy ... to shake a man's faith in himself. To take advantage of that, to break a man's spirit, is devil's work.
—GEORGE BERNARD SHAW

I think many of us are unaware of the damage we do, the swath we cut, when we demand others do as we do.

"Why isn't Smith at his desk?"
"Where is that report? I needed it an hour ago!"
"Can't she get sick on her own time?"
"He's not really committed to his job. If he were he'd have shown up on Sunday, like I did."

Workaholics need partners in their crimes. And they're everywhere. Fear is the key, and power drives the car. There are plenty of victims out there, and we must be careful not to invite them into our dens.

.~.

I will be alert about how I treat others. I will not ask them to overextend themselves because I do. I will be careful not to break their spirit.

Better to write for yourself and have no public than to write for the public and have no self.
—CYRIL CONNOLLY

Men who do too much are constantly trying to please others. Our self-images are in tatters; we have low self-esteem and that's why we hide behind the work we create.

What is left of us if all we do, we do to please others? How do we define ourselves? What happens to our lives, and who is there to catch us when we fall?

The effort in pleasing the public far outweighs the rewards for having done so. And finally, the fraudulent inability of having served the public leaves us with catastrophic consequences.

.~.

I do not want to be lost in a sea of demands, of self-creation that is fiction. I want to act as myself, for myself.

Unhappiness is best described as the difference between our talents and our expectations.
—EDWARD DE BONO

Men who work too much expect too much; from themselves, mostly, but also from everyone around them. We may be talented, intelligent, and creative, but our expectations often blunt our attributes, throwing a hazy camouflage over the very things we're good at.

And can depression be far behind? No, because we never live up to *our* expectations for ourselves. We invite unhappiness when we demand too much of ourselves. They go hand in hand.

∿

I can always tell when I'm about to go into a depression. It's easy, because it's always at a time when my plate is too full, I've promised too much, and I'd have to be three people to deliver. I will try to break this pattern.

Human beings are perhaps never more frightening than when they are convinced beyond doubt that they are right. —LAURENS VAN DER POST

When I'm deep in my disease I'm also at my most inflexible. But I also believe that, in part at least, this inflexibility and unwavering feeling of always being "right" or "justified" comes from a long-term depression.

When we grow up constantly confronted by harsh, demanding questions, questions that create self-doubt, forcing us always to try to "measure up" to the standards of others (or, at least, not behave like a defective adult), we can never feel "good enough."

We become rigid in our self-expectations, demanding—and getting—more and more from ourselves. What other overriding emotion can we come away with except depression?

∼

Very often there is no one right answer. There are many. Today, and in future days, I will try to be flexible in my thoughts and my expectations. I know that will help with my depression.

It is not enough to succeed. Others must fail.
—GORE VIDAL

In many cases it is the failures of our parents that shaped our success. Thus, our self-image is, at least in part, based on the inabilities and shortcomings of others.

To feel good about our own lawn, we have to look across the fence and see our neighbor's weeds. And what if we don't? What if the balance shifts, and it looks like the other fellow is doing better than we are? We take on more than we can handle. The irony is that then we really do begin to fail. Our prized efficiency erodes, our priorities go unfulfilled, we begin to judge ourselves too harshly, and finally, we become "the others who fail."

．～．

Life at its best is not about competing. It is about enjoying. Today I will try not to get into a competitive situation and set myself up for the ultimate self-failure.

This book is about the organization man ... I can think of no other way to describe the people I am talking about. They are not the workers, nor are they the white-collar people in the usual, dark sense of the word. These people only work for the organization. The mess I am talking about belongs *to it as well.*
   —WILLIAM H. WHYTE, JR.

When we have a poor self-image and need to look elsewhere for assurance that we are OK or superior, we are in trouble. If I cannot look inward, delve into myself for answers, begin to decide who I am *for myself,* then I become someone who allows himself to be invaded, to be designed and fashioned by others, most often my peers and superiors at work. When I do this, my career becomes me. I become the organization man—a husk of who I *can* be.

~

I am far more than my work, and I refuse to be defined by it. I will remember that I am a person with many facets and that I have a great deal to offer myself and others.

Literature is strewn with the wreckage of men who have minded beyond reason the opinions of others.
—VIRGINIA WOOLF

What makes us run so far, so fast, leaving little energy left for anything we really want to do?

Maybe, at least in part, it's because we're too eager to please, racing toward someone else's standards. Whether these false standards and demands were set by our fathers, our wives' fathers, or by the men and women for whom we work, we are too aware of the opinions and the tests others put to us and to our abilities and talents.

～

I must learn to trust my opinions and pay less attention to those of others, some of whom have designed theirs to trip me up or make me fail.

Children have never been very good at listening to their elders, but they have never failed to imitate them. They must, they have no other models.
—JAMES BALDWIN

Whether the teacher is our father or mother or professor or clergy, we learned our most basic, and later ingrained, social behaviors from what they showed to us, not what they said to us.

As children, we imitate behaviors, good and bad. We develop patterns of coping by virtue of how we see our elders cope. If our father learned to cope by canceling his feelings and running away from confrontation, then we too learn that behavior and almost certainly repeat it.

.∼.

I must always be mindful that it is not only my words that my children hear, but how hard I slam a door and how calmly I approach their failures.

Under the conditions of tyranny, it is far easier to act than to think. —HANNAH ARENDT

If you've ever worked in a setting where demand runs way beyond reason, where anger and lack of trust abound, then you've probably acted, reacted, and overreacted to the pain of that kind of tyranny.

Men who do too much are often getting their paychecks from a tyrannical boss. And as surely as they carry that paycheck home, they carry with it the same kind of tyranny and bestow it on the family.

·~·

I will try to break the cycle of tyranny, not bring the vestiges of it to my partner, my children, and others whom I love.

Well, here's another fine mess you've gotten me into.
—OLIVER HARDY TO STAN LAUREL

Laurel and Hardy were the first male codependents captured on film. As funny as they were, they worked together like a lighted match and a powder keg.

How often have we said to our lovers and partners, "Well, here's another fine mess you've gotten me into"? Blame comes naturally for those of us who do too much. And the more we take on, the more fault we must find with those around us who "got us into this mess."

Laurel and Hardy didn't know about "keeping it simple." They only knew how to dig the hole deeper and deeper until they couldn't peer over the mounds of dirt they'd shoveled over their shoulders!

.~.

Words of blame. Easy to say, they trip off the tongue more easily than just about anything else. Since it gets me no further to blame others and makes me not a bit happier, I'll try to look only to myself for the answers to my problems.

We are effectively destroying ourselves by violence masquerading as love. —R. D. LAING

Fear breeds violence—both physical and psychological—in relationships. I've seen so many men who, because they fear they will lose the one they love so much, in the end destroy them.

Men who do too much are riddled with fear. We need to examine where our fear comes from and what it is doing to us, and finally, if it is causing us to create the kind of psychological violence in our relationships that masquerades as love.

～

Love is not controlling. Love is not violating someone else's choices. Unilateral control is a form of violence. Today I will try to understand why I have the need to control others, and how that need is hurting me.

I think I can fit you in on my calendar in April . . .
1995, I mean. —ANONYMOUS

More than once, on a Friday afternoon, looking at my
calendar for the following week, I've actually thought
that there was no room for a slip-up, a mistake, or a
surprise in the next seven days. I'm already so overcommitted that if something shows up postage due
on Tuesday, it will throw the whole week off.

～

I am trying very hard to leave large gaps of "unscheduled" time on my calendar. It has helped clear
my head. I feel no dread about my calendar and I find
I get more done when less is scheduled.

When elephants fight, it is the grass that suffers.
—AFRICAN PROVERB

When men who have great impact—some directly, some less so—on other people, it is often those lower on the ladder who suffer the most from those big men in the boardroom who make the decisions.

How helpless so many of us have felt when our "superiors" behaved without ethics, without plans, without direction, but with one giant and final thunderbolt from the blue—and we were left to suffer the consequences.

Wars are planned by generals; but it is the soldiers who die on distant fields.

. .

Men who know only combat in work always forget those who are most affected by their battles. Those of us who are in positions of authority and power need to be reminded of how far the echoes of our tyrannies can be heard, and by whom.

Either this man is dead or my watch has stopped.
  —GROUCHO MARX

Not so fast, Groucho. What about daydreaming?

We've never been told, at least by anyone we really trust, that being idle, if only for moments at a time, is just as valuable as moving, making decisions, performing for the sake of making us feel that we're doing "our share"—or more than our share.

I'd much prefer to watch a man contemplating a decision than acting out and thinking later.

·~·

There's value in quiet contemplation. It's rejuvenating. It's an act of self-respect, and finally, an act of respect for those whose lives we touch.

*For three days after death, hair and fingernails continue
to grow but phone calls taper off.*
   —JOHNNY CARSON

I'm not so sure. I don't think certain people I know
would take death as an excuse not to call or expect
a return call. Or a fax. These days, we could substi-
tute the word "fax" for "phone calls" in Carson's
quote and be more accurate.

In this day of instant communication, everything
constitutes an emergency. The fax machine has made
a passing, vague question a cause for immediate attention. We need to learn the difference between
what is important enough to insist on someone else's
immediate attention and what can wait for a return
letter or a conversation over lunch.

Someday I will want to say, "Unplug everything
but my pacemaker!"

．～．

A question that needs an answer should be important enough to get the attention it deserves. I will not
telephone thirty-five times, fax thirty-seven times, to
get someone's attention. I will not be the boy who
cried, "Fax!"

I don't want any yes-men around me. I want everybody to tell me the truth, even if it costs them their jobs.
—SAMUEL GOLDWYN

At least he was up front about it. Goldwyn ran the most profitable movie studio in the world for decades, even if he was the West Coast king of the malapropism.

It is very hard always to tell the truth, not to fall into the pleaser's rut. All of us want to be a success, to be liked, respected, and admired for what we do.

When we take a close look at ourselves and see that our dishonesties have gotten us where we are, that's when it's time to take an even harder, more discerning look at who we've become and who we're really trying to please.

.~.

Telling the truth does, indeed, set us free. The volume of lies we tell in order to put up a better front only diminishes us in the end.

A man can't get rich if he takes proper care of his family.
—NAVAJO SAYING

What are our priorities? To be admired, feared, or held high by the public? To be the richest, most powerful man in town? To have the biggest BMW on the block?

Who will end up taking care of us when we need tending? Not the car and not the public.

Our families, our partners, our extended families, our children will always be there for us if we can make the decision to be there for them.

.~.

I have lived long enough and made enough mistakes to know that my belongings are of secondary significance to me. I do know that I have lost time with my children because I haven't always been clear about the source of my riches.

My grandfather used to make home movies and edit out the joy. —RICHARD LEWIS

Men who do too much don't laugh a lot. That's because there are tasks to be done, projects to be designed, things to be accomplished. After all, the whole family will go down in flames if I'm not hard at work keeping it together. And what's the fun in that? It's hard work to make others happy and we certainly don't have time, nor do we deserve to be happy ourselves.

When we're constantly afraid of something gaining on us, the fear controls us totally. Laughter is suspect, joy an emotion to be avoided at all costs.

.~.

Ever hear people say, "Oh well, Christmas is for kids anyway!?" Translated, that means, "Grow up. Don't be joyful or gleeful if you're past ten years old." Men who do too much need to kick back and get silly. If we're lucky, we still have someone around to get silly with.

Half the people in America are faking it.
—ROBERT MITCHUM

And the other half?

When I worked for a major entertainment corporation I always thought at least half of the employees were faking it. *And getting away with it!*

But what was I doing? Working hard. Too hard. Answering to certain people senior to me in management and junior to me in intellect. Then spending precious hours commuting to a suburb outside the city to a life-style that was outrageously over my head financially. So, who was faking it, anyway?

Now I'm working for myself. I have my own business. Now if I fake it, I'll know in a minute. Or at least I try to.

~

I'll go look in the mirror and think about what I'm faking and what I'm doing that's real for me, what makes me proud, makes me laugh, and makes me sleep soundly at night.

I am the kind of paranoiac in reverse. I suspect people of plotting to make me happy.   —J. D. SALINGER

Few of us would be described as "happy" guys. Those who love us are always trying to bring us around. First they engage in the same overcommitted behavior that we are involved in. Then they try the opposite tact—attempting to enjoy life by slowing their pace. Then, when neither of those stances work, and there are no more defenses, no more charades, they abandon us.

All that simply because someone dared to love us, to make us happy, to empower us to love them. So much of our compulsive behaviors are unconscious, but those who are plotting to make us happy may not know that.

~.

I will try to understand the actions of those who want me to be more present with them and hear that they want to see me happy.

There are very few people who don't become more interesting when they stop talking.
—MARY LOWRY

Men who do too much often talk too much. We simply think much of what we say will be unthinkably fascinating to just about everybody.

It is difficult to be humble when you're overcommitted. After all, it was, in some respects, a lack of being humble that made us "big enough" to accept assignment after promise after job.

Many of us talk about what we are doing rather than do what we're talking about.

Many of us are poor listeners. We need to hear what others think, what others need, what it is that others truly want of us.

Today, and for days beyond, I will try to listen more than I talk. I want to learn from others, not just hear the echo of my overcommitments.

MAY 1

Great moments in science: Einstein discovers time is actually money. —GARY LARSON

That's an equation all of us understand.

When I was growing up, one of the cruelest and most frequently heard words was *procrastination*. My self-worth became totally bound up in whether I was procrastinating or getting something done. Was I "accomplishing" anything? Or was I being a kid, doing kid things, without a lot of regard for the calendar or the clock or something that would eventually add up to something—most likely, money?

And, anyway, if time equals money, what does the lack of time equal?

∼

Today, I'll carve out some time, not for money, but for fun. Pure and simple.

No man can think clearly when his fists are clenched.
—GEORGE JEAN NATHAN

So many of us are constantly uptight, afraid, angry, ready for anything, poised on the brink of a fight. We're tight and our physical posture shows it.

When we're at our worst, our fists are clenched, we grind our teeth, and we have no patience. And our thinking is clouded by all of this. We see everyone as an impediment, or worse, an enemy. Our thought processes are virtually at a standstill, our wires crossed and soldered with free-floating anxiety and aimless anger. We're literally at our own throats.

～

There are real enemies and there are imagined enemies. In order to sort them out we must first investigate ourselves. Today I will attempt to untie the binds of my anxiety and unclench my fists.

Nice guys finish last, but we get to sleep in.
  —EVAN DAVIS

Who said life was one big race? Who really cares who comes in first anyway? Too many of us get professional sports mixed up with our professions. Competition in life, in all aspects of it, is totally draining. It leaves us without any emotional or intellectual reserves.

What's the deal with speed? Does everything have to be measured? Calibrated? How many miles did you run? How long did it take you? How fast does your car go? Did you get there first? Why can't we just run the marathon for the exercise?

Nice or not, I don't want to be measured by my peers or by myself every time I undertake a project, at work or at home.

~

I won't compare my performance today against anyone else's. I'll work or play at my pace.

The trouble with life in the fast lane is that you get to the other end in an awful hurry.   —JOHN JENSEN

So far, I've lived life in the fast lane, the middle lane, and the exit lane. Not simultaneously, of course. I lived a number of years in the fast lane, and the truth is, I don't remember much about it. Some of it was fun, I'm sure, but the windburn caused me to slow down.

I was in the fast lane so long that I tried the exit lane, which doesn't really work, of course, especially if you have children to help take care of. And the exit lane takes you off the road altogether, which isn't realistic, either.

I often wonder if the friends and business acquaintances who were in the fast lane along with me remember much more than I do about the scenery. I think many of them are still there because they don't know there's another way of living.

.~.

I'm going to begin taking life at the pace I think my body and mind were designed for.

Sometimes a scream is better than a thesis.
—RALPH WALDO EMERSON

There are times—and most of us have felt this more than once—when a verbal document, a reasoned, intelligent conversation, is useless, because we need the catharsis that a scream can give us.

Sometimes there are just too many memos, too much discussion, too many meetings, and once in a while we need to scream out to get *our own* attention.

When the wind tunnel of reason just shuts us off, we need the piercing scream that signals that we've gone too far.

·~·

Men who do too much do too much reasoning and live in quiet, but fantastically busy, desperation. Before I scream, I'll attempt to stop and look at what I've created and what I've left behind.

The trouble with the rat race is that even if you win you're still a rat. —LILY TOMLIN

We spend our days in the same office building, or airport hanger, or high school gymnasium, or maybe we're working two or three jobs. We are called by many names: bricklayer, doctor, messenger, or accountant. But we're still all only men and we're capable of just so much.

We can do only what is possible, and we need to examine what that is. For some men it is different than for others. But when all is said and done, we are more alike than unalike. Whether we want to hear that or not, it should be some source of comfort.

I am not very different from the man waiting in front of me on line, nor from the man waiting behind. I need to remind myself of that today.

The richer your friends, the more they will cost you.
—ELISABETH MARBURY

If I tried to keep up with some of the people I do business with, I'd be bankrupt tomorrow before the banks opened.

My friends and clients do not mean to inflict their wealth on me, indeed they don't. I, however, must be sure that I don't inflict their wealth on me.

My expectations regarding where I can live, where I can vacation, what schools my children can attend, what I can afford to drive are not dictated by what my friends can afford in each instance.

But there are days when I have to fight the urge to spend up to what my bloated sense of self-expectation is. So I try.

❦

Today I will not make excuses either to myself or to others, that I cannot (or will not) afford what they can.

The graveyards are full of indispensable men.
—CHARLES DE GAULLE

What a wonderful quote. It helps me to read it just before I go on vacation or take a day or even an afternoon off. Or anytime I think I might be indispensable.

While contemplating buying more life insurance the other day, I said to my wife, "I think we should increase it a great deal." She responded, "I'm not helpless. If something happens to you I'll be able to make enough money. This increase is frivolous and expensive."

But if I'm not here, shouldn't she have a couple of million dollars to tide her over? That way I could be responsible even after I'm dead.

.~.

I need to remember we've all got a one-way ticket and all those important men went out without the right coverage to prevent death.

I have never liked working. To me, a job is an invasion of privacy. —DANNY MCGOORTY

A job can certainly be that. We were taught to go to school and then get a good job (and a couple of other things along the way, too). But what is a good job? One that doesn't feel like an invasion of privacy?

If we find something we love to do, as the well-known book title suggests, "the money will follow." I pretty much believe that. I'm *not* talking about endless amounts of self-esteem and involvement born out of a "job" you love.

What are you talking about?

.~.

I need to discover what "work" is. It needn't be just a "job." It really can be something, or part of something that I'm pretty passionate about.

Men who never get carried away should be.
—MALCOLM FORBES

Many of us don't let go easily. We don't know how to let our guard down long enough to really get silly, get carried away, get nuts, and forget about the stack of work on the desk or the workbench or the machine shop.

Our children, if we're lucky enough to have some, can be great teachers for those of us who take everything too seriously. Get silly with them. Roll around and let yourself be touched, literally and figuratively. Tell some crazy jokes. Make some faces. Don't worry, be happy (at least for a bit).

～

Find some kids, even if they're not your own, and play some games on the floor or in the yard, and you may not look at the clock until the first child yawns.

The two hardest things in life are failure and success.
—UNKNOWN

Sometimes it's difficult to discern which is which. Yes, that's flippant, but what we commonly call failure can lead to what we commonly call success.

We need to stop thinking in absolutes. Is there absolute failure, absolute success? Is there only black and white? I don't think that is the healthy way to view our performance in anything we do.

My friend Harvey, when asked where he placed in the New York marathon, answered, "First place." "First place!" exclaimed our mutual friend incredulously. Harvey said, "Just running and finishing the race, in my mind, brought me in first."

Our lives and our work are an interrelated chain of events and performances. As we live a life, a mosaic is created. There are modulations in color, in line, in texture, nuance in coincidence of edge, and perspective. There is no absolute failure, no absolute success.

~

If I live my days one day at a time, I can often have a fulfilling and pleasing day. If I race against an imaginary clock, for an imaginary prize, toward an imaginary end zone, I will never be fulfilled.

I'm trying to arrange my life so that I don't even have to be present.   —UNKNOWN

All of us like to hide out. The trouble is some of us only like to hide out. We'd delegate breathing if it were possible.

Hiding can be healthy, but it can also be bad for us. If we use too much camouflage, those we care about cannot find us. We're nonentities, lost on purpose. Of course, when you hide you don't have to take part in life.

Many of us hide out in our calendars, or at sports events, on airplanes, rushing from one metro area to another, one board meeting to another, keeping in touch via our precious cellular phones. Never out of reach, but never within reach.

.~.

Those of us who hide, who aren't present, are missing just about everything—especially growth. Today I'll be more forthcoming, more approachable, more present for those who love me and for those I love.

I never know how much of what I say is true.
—BETTE MIDLER

When you talk real fast and never come up for air long enough for anyone else to cram in a word or a thought edgewise, you sure can get lost in your own rhetoric.

This happens with great regularity to those of us who feel that others depend on us for guidance, indeed for their existence. We have so carefully constructed our self-myths that sometimes we believe them. The only trouble is we're one thing one day, another the next. We need a script just to remember our lines.

We need to slow down, listen to what we are saying and what we're not saying. We need to be present at our own podiums, our own speeches. And men who do too much love to entertain, so we've got to watch out for that, too.

ᐧᐧ

I'll be conscious today of how much I need to say as opposed to how much I want to say.

People don't change their careers; they're engulfed by them. —JOHN DOS PASSOS

More and more that is the truth. In the age of the Concorde, the fax, carry-on cellular phones and carry-on luggage, we've lost sight of why we chose our "careers" in the first place. Even worse, it becomes almost unimaginable to change.

When do we know our careers are overtaking us? When we think about them far more than we think about our children, our partners, our parents, our lovers, ourselves. When we are no longer kind and giving because we have forgotten how to be. When we start to live out of fear rather than choice. When we begin to hide in our offices or behind our newspapers. Or when we medicate ourselves with beer or food.

.~.

I will be mindful of what I can control as opposed to what is about to control me. I will attempt to take an important inventory today.

Life is an adventure in forgiveness.
—NORMAN COUSINS

Oh, yes. This is an area I find most of the overcommitted have trouble with.

How do you begin? Who do you begin with? So many tell me they first think of their fathers—the ones who they learned the most from. The ones who taught them, inadvertently, that being a "hard worker and good provider" was everything. That, if necessary, you work two, maybe three jobs to pay the bills. That you put off the vacations, you come home late, and you need that second, third, or fifth drink just to clear your mind for sleep.

Men who do too much first need to learn to forgive themselves—for what we believe are our great failures.

And then forgive another.

.~.

Today I will take some time to attempt to trace the road that brought me here. I need to forgive myself for using that route, but I need to learn why I took it.

*When it comes time to do your own life, you either
perpetuate your childhood or you stand on it and finally
kick it out from under.* —ROSELLEN BROWN

Rosellen Brown's quote is great, even out of context.
I once heard a variation on this thought that said that
our marriages were fought on the battlefields that
once were our playgrounds. A little silly in a way, but
it does speak to growing up, growing away, making
amends, forgiving, and moving on.

So many of us do not know how to say good-
bye—to our lovers, to our friends, to jobs that have
failed us and vice versa, to our children as they grow
up, or finally, to our own childhoods. So we busy
ourselves in the act of being very tall children, acting
out, and never coming to terms with the pains, frustrations, or disappointments we endured as children.

⋅∼⋅

Today I'm going to look at those childhood behaviors I've carried through my adult life with an eye to
kicking those support systems out from under me.

I don't know the key to success, but the key to failure is trying to please everybody. —BILL COSBY

That's about the size of it. Most of us are trying to please everybody, and all of the time. It starts with our parents, mostly our fathers. Then our teachers, maybe our ministers or our rabbis. Then we try to please our friends—we've done ridiculous things trying to please our friends. And then we try to please our employers or our professors or our counselors or our new-found lovers.

And the oddest thing keeps happening: the more we try to please them, hold on to them, keep them laughing, applauding, hugging, and holding us, the more we fail them. It's because we're never "whole" with them, we're only with them for the moment, never for the long run. So every time we try to please them the only way we know how (or *think* we know how), we fail. And fail again.

~.

First, I need to please myself, make myself whole and happy. Today I'll try to think about all the ways I might do that.

Men of power have no time to read; yet the men who do not read are unfit for power. —MICHAEL FOOT

So many of us make decisions quickly and that makes us feel like we're efficient and smart. But where do we get the information needed to make rapid decisions? Since most of us are too busy to read the whole daily newspaper, any trade magazines, or a book for pleasure, what is the source of our information?

Most men who do too much also, of course, do too little. Too little of a lot of things. Reading, of course, is one of those things. If we read for pleasure, it's suspect. If we read for work, we may view that as a waste of time, too, because it's not an "activity"—it appears passive.

∿

I will begin reading and informing myself about my work, but today I will also find something to read that I will truly enjoy.

Competing pressures tempt one to believe that an issue deferred is a problem avoided; more often it is a crisis invented. —HENRY KISSINGER

How well we hide away at our desks, at our work. If we successfully put off the confrontation of competing problems, we dupe ourselves into believing that we've bought time and then won a battle. But we really know that we've created, at least most of the time, a greater, less manageable problem that will pop up again. We create crisis by avoiding it as best we can. With our heads bowed over our work and our brows furrowed, we look just like we're handling everything, even when we're not.

.~.

Today, I will not create diversions. I will meet the problems and issues as they arise, and not put them off.

*It's no accident many accuse me of conducting public
affairs with my heart instead of my head. Well, what if I
do? . . . Those who don't know how to weep with their
whole heart don't know how to laugh either.*
   —GOLDA MEIR

I've often felt that what is commonly thought of as a
female trait, that of nurturing, is actually conducive
to managing people, getting them on task, keeping
them focused, and getting a job "done." I'd like to
think men can adopt this trait, at least some portion
of it, and learn to manage more with their hearts and
less with their heads and hands.

   Golda Meir was an astonishingly strong leader,
perhaps, in part, because she led with her whole
being intact. She didn't deny herself joy or grief, and
because of that as much as anything she won respect
from millions of people throughout the world.

❦

Today I'll attempt to see those with whom I work
with my heart. I want to look into them, not at them.
I believe it will help me to respect them and in turn
respect myself.

Man is only truly great when he acts from the passions.
—BENJAMIN DISRAELI

We lose sight of our passions when we overwork.
Sometimes we are really escaping our passion by
overcommitting. On purpose.

My greatest passion was painting. I gave it up
because I didn't think it would be viewed as a serious
"career." An artist is always suspected of cheating
life. Artists cannot be measured in traditional ways.
Most artists don't make a lot of money.

Strange, isn't it? I gave it up because I thought I
was cheating. Turns out I was cheating myself by not
sticking with it. I can feel it almost daily.

.~.

Today I will take some time to at least investigate
one of my passions and maybe I'll focus on it enough
so that it gives me pleasure, not remorse.

Power is not happiness   —WILLIAM GODWIN

So many of us are ensnared and intoxicated by the idea of power: We believe that if we can attain a certain level of power, we will be free of tyranny.

However, power for its own sake brings no relief, no solace, no happiness. It is the way in which we use our power that can make us content, but few of us take account of what power will afford us or how we intend to use it, because we are too focused on attaining it for the sake of having it.

·~·

Today I shall inventory my need for power in order to discover what is behind my drive to attain it.

Men are not prisoners of fate, but only prisoners of their own minds. —FRANKLIN D. ROOSEVELT

We don't wake up every morning with the house on fire. But we act like it. We're frantic. We're busy. We're prisoners of the time card, the time clock, the expressways, the slow elevators, the busy telephones, the relentless, towering In Box.

When we stop believing that the world is trying to do us in—that this is our lot in life, that fate dealt us too many cards—and when we start being accountable for our feelings, thoughts, and actions, we break the cycle that held us prisoner. A man who takes the time to think and know his own mind will never be held against his true will.

~

Today I'll think about the possibilities of life—not my self-imposed limitations.

There is more to life than increasing its speed.
—MAHATMA GANDHI

The time it takes to complete a task, any task, is of the utmost interest to men who do too much.

Move. Faster. Faster. Get it done. "Ahead of schedule" is music to our ears. "On time" is OK, but "before deadline" almost makes us swoon.

Velocity covers an enormous lack of self-awareness. If we can slow down enough to know what we're doing and why we're doing it, our lives begin to stabilize and we begin to see far beyond our tasks.

∿

I will let a natural rhythm become my metronome today. I will not rush headlong and empty-headed into every task at hand.

I have a new philosophy. I'm only going to dread one day at a time. —CHARLES M. SCHULZ

Charles Schulz is a clever man. He's proven it in his millions of Peanuts® cartoon strips, through his characters and their situations and personalities. He's made us laugh, but he's made us think, too.

Work-dependent men do dread each day at a time. But we also dread each week and each month. We think that next week's empty calendar will allow us to catch up on everything so that by the end of the week, we can leave the office empty-handed and free as a bird. Yet we always seem to manage to fill up the next week and the week after that . . .

◆

Today I will look at only what I can manage today. I will not look at the whole desk, I will look at what I think I can master. No more.

Living with a saint is more grueling than being one.
—ROBERT NEVILLE

I often wondered how other men I worked with had empty desks at the end of the day. They always set a terrible example for me. Some of these guys really did get their work done on time and did it well.

I was noticeably more verbal, more quick-witted, and often caustic in the office. But what was really valued, of course, were the guys whose desks were neat or empty at five P.M. each day.

I knew some of these guys had to be a mass of hysteria within. But it galled me that on the outside all was well. I wanted their desks to reflect their inner turmoil.

~·~

In my process of recovery, I will try not to lord my healing over those who have not yet attained my understanding of this disease.

After all is said and done, more is said than done.
—UNKNOWN

Meetings. Caucuses. Committees. Group discussions. Talk. More talk. I think so many of us believe what we say because it makes us think we've actually accomplished a task.

Work-dependent men love to talk about the work they're so engrossed in—but only in terms of the crosses they bear because of it.

One corporation I worked within actually had so many meetings scheduled each day that very often, I and others would not get back to our respective desks until after five P.M. This left us the evening to return calls. That's fine if you're doing business with LA and you're in New York. Otherwise it poses quite a problem.

～

Today I will try and be succinct in what I say. But I will not fill up the balance of the day as a nonverbal taskmaster.

Correct me if I'm wrong, but hasn't the fine line between sanity and madness gotten finer?
—GEORGE PRICE

There's a major new opinion poll about everything you can think of every other day. And all of us are expected to keep up with all of it.

But us workaholics secretly love this overabundance of information. We love this overload of useless data because it helps support our disease.

I was proud to announce publicly once that I read four newspapers daily. Wow! And returned forty or fifty phone calls. Gee!

And then what?

᠅

I do not care what Madonna did yesterday, and today I'll focus on what I know to be important. I'll try not to blur-out on sound bites.

WARNING TO ALL PERSONNEL: *Firings will continue until morale improves.*   —UNKNOWN

Isn't fear great? For the past several thousand years it's been proven that you don't get anything really good out of people by scaring them into it. And you cannot build a healthy organization, be it a corporation or a family, on the basis of fear.

But so many of us engage in this type of insane manipulation. Those of us who carry too much of the burden (happily, just ask), are often given to fear tactics.

It takes courage to be kind. It takes introspection and thought. Tyranny is easy.

∿

Today I will examine how I speak to everyone. I will be conscious not to belittle or condescend. I know kindness works.

If it weren't for the last minute, nothing would get done.
—UNKNOWN

There are all kinds of work addicts out there. The way their disease works is manifested in a myriad of ways.

But a favorite, and probably the most prevalent, is the last-minute guy. The eleventh hour is the only time that anything really gets done. There's talk, there's anguish, there's hand-wringing, there's planning, and then bingo, as if from left field, comes the—drumroll—deadline!

It seems impossible to us last-minute men. We sweated, we talked, we gave it everything, and now we're in danger of being late with the goods!

Today I will think about pacing myself, and will not wait until the last minute to finish my work, or anything I promise.

Fanaticism consists of redoubling your effort when you have forgotten your aim. —GEORGE SANTAYANA

Sometimes we work ourselves into such a state that we become fanatics. We lose sight of what our goals are, and we rush ahead for the sake of getting there first. But where is "there"?

"Getting there," as the Cunard Line slogan used to say, "is half the fun." But it's more than that. Getting there is half the process, but you must not forget where you're headed. Producing steam simply produces humidity.

•~•

I will be clear about my goals and not let the fear of not finishing first enter the picture.

Start every day off with a smile and get it over with.
—W. C. FIELDS

I have a lot of respect for a man who is up front with himself and in tune with others.

So many of us think that we have to wear a mask of happiness, a cheerful expression, in order to please everybody. Many of us who are overcommitted are so because we're busy attempting to appease someone else.

We need to work to get to a place where we can be sincere and honest, where we're comfortable doing what we can do, and not wear the frozen mask of the superhuman.

◆

Today I'll be aware of how I really feel, and not try to adopt someone else's idea of how I should feel.

During a carnival, men put masks over their masks.
—XAVIER FORNERET

Sometimes it's hard to get to the center of a man, to find out who he really is. Is it because he is too frightened to show his true self to another? Is it because he has worn the mask so long that he only feels comfortable with it on?

It is hard work to dismantle a mask within a mask within a mask. But in order to do our work, and untangle the reasons we have for carrying the burdens we carry, then we have to attempt to get to the center of who we are.

◆

I will be especially mindful today of not working incognito. I want to display to everyone who I really am.

Never keep up with the Joneses. Drag them down to your level. —QUENTIN CRISP

I'm amazed at how, even totally immersed in work, we can be aware of what the other guy has. It's almost as though we had a third eye. This eye is trained on the neighbors, on our coworkers, anybody who might be getting a slightly larger slice of pie than we've got.

Competition has always been a problem for us. We compete with ourselves because we learned to compete for love and attention when we were children. And we never have enough. Our glass is always half empty. And filling our days and nights is our way of trying to fill the glass to the top.

.~.

I will do my best to pay attention to my needs, not take on the needs of others, and be careful not to need what others have.

A lie would make no sense, unless the truth were felt to be dangerous. —CARL JUNG

We tell ourselves and others, if we can get away with it, that we are in control, that everything is OK. We hunger for control, to lose the feeling that everything is just beyond us, and that we're caught up in a self-made cyclone.

The truth is that we lie to one another, to ourselves, to our wives, to our children, to our partners, and to our friends. The truth is we are hiding something dangerous. It's our addiction to work, our addiction to promise, and our gigantic need to cover for our sickness.

~·

Today, when I feel the overload of responsibility, I will look at it for what it is: self-imposed. I will not feel ashamed, but I do need to be aware of what I am doing to myself.

*If I had to live my life again, I'd make the same
mistakes, only sooner.* —TALLULAH BANKHEAD

We not only make mistakes, but we repeat them
endlessly.

To make changes takes too much time. To make
choices uses up valuable energy. So we repeat the
past, even if it's not worth repeating. We use the
same old script rather than take the time to write a
new one.

I think Tallulah Bankhead's message really means
more than it seems at first. I think implied in the
sarcasm is the hope that she would learn from those
early mistakes, thus allowing the rest of her life more
balance, making it less terrifying.

∿·

Because I don't have my life to live over, I will be
more aware of what I'm doing with this one. I do not
want to make the same mistakes and will be more
vigilant in taking care of myself.

All phone calls are obscene.
—KAREN ELIZABETH GORDON

There are days, maybe most days, that we feel this way. Men who do too much believe that, even in business, we are being invaded by telephone calls. But we're also proud of all those telephone messages! They're like badges of honor, those little pink slips. "I'm the most busy, the most harassed, the most in demand," these little pieces of paper tell us.

The paradox is, of course, that even though we hate the phone calls and find them oppressive, they become symbols of our success—and actually help define our self-worth! A very crazy place to be.

~

I've taken to sorting my phone messages into these piles: those that need returning as soon as possible and those that can wait. All of us know which is which.

I always turn to the sports pages first, which record people's accomplishments. The front page has nothing but man's failures. —CHIEF JUSTICE EARL WARREN

I'm not certain the sports pages don't carry a few stories about men's failures, too, but I certainly get his point.

So many of us work-addicted men are heavily involved in sports. I'm talking about spectator sports, of course. Sports scores, statistics, we know them all. Many of us hide behind the sports pages, the sports magazines, and the sports channels and never come out. Maybe it's due in part to arrested development, but mostly I think it's the only way we know how to relate to one another and to ourselves.

The proliferation of sports radio talk shows is frightening. So now, to and from work, many of us can be medicated some more by endless discussion of the latest score, trade, or sports blunder.

Today I will try reading some other parts of the newspaper, pay attention to other kinds of news, and put my love and overinvolvement in sports in perspective.

JUNE 8

Start slow and taper off. —WALT STACK

Pace. We don't know about this. Pacing ourselves so that by ten-thirty in the morning, after a potful of coffee and a half pack of cigarettes, we're ready to call it a day.

In sick organizations, output and fervent pace are demanded. So what do we do? Quit our jobs? Try and change the organization? Tell our bosses to ease up?

Yes. We look for work that allows us to be human. We think about careers that allow for natural growth, reward, celebration. We stop allowing others to point to us with a stopwatch. We need to take responsibility for our work in a new way, and discover what the expectations of that business are as opposed to our own.

～

I will stop complaining about my work load. If it is "impossible" to deal with, then I need to remove myself and find a place that respects balanced people who can contribute to it.

You might as well fall flat on your face as lean over too far backward.   —JAMES THURBER

When our commitments cause great strain, we eventually do just that—fall on our faces. When we see that we're overprocessed, we're in up to our ears, we need to stop and take note of the water line and what all of this is costing us.

If we're winning so much in one area, surely we're losing in others. Show me a man who has made several million dollars in a few years by being absent from home and I'll show you a man without a family, without friends, who is virtually alone with his cash and who eventually will find himself flat on his face.

∿

Give, give, give. Till it hurts. Who told us that? Where'd we pick that up? Today is a day to make a decision about how much I can give, as opposed to how much I feel I must give.

Only the mediocre are always at their best.
  —JEAN GIRAUDOUX

We must allow for variances in our performances, in our modes, in our "output." As humans, we are capable of a great deal, but not every day.

Perfection addiction, as Dr. Anne Wilson Schaef says, is just as quick a route to self-annihilation as a gun to the head.

We need to allow ourselves to fail, to fall, to do nothing; to think and to excel only when we have the energy to excel.

And we need not shame ourselves for not always winning, bringing home the pennant, or cashing the big check.

━◦━

Today I need not judge myself by someone else's standards. I will do what I can do.

For people who like peace and quiet: A phoneless cord.
—UNKNOWN

I don't know about you, but I'd probably rush to buy one of those.

We really don't need to be tyrannized by the telephone, the fax, the U.S. mail, or Overnight Express. We need to discover, for ourselves, what is important enough to pay attention to now!

So many of us behave as though we work in the emergency room of an understaffed hospital in a battle zone. Every day is an emergency! What to do first? Who's bleeding the most? Who needs CPR? How fast can I get an X ray?

With all due respect for the men and women who do work in that setting, I think the rest of us ought to look on them with wonder and awe and be happy we don't work in that environment.

Today I'll not allow the telephone to dictate my day. After all, it is my telephone.

The higher the monkey climbs, the more you see of its behind. —GENERAL JOSEPH STILWELL

Moving up that ladder of success, as fast as our arms and legs can carry us, without acknowledging who or what is in our way, exposes us as workaholics like nothing else.

We need to examine why we're on the ladder in the first place. What's at the top? Do we really know? And what's on the ladder in between the top and, say, the middle?

Is it money that drives us up so high so fast? Lack of self-esteem? Shame for being forty and not making "enough" money? Are we trying to show our fathers or wives or lovers just what extraordinary people we are?

～

The monkey that hurries too fast not only shows his behind, but most probably falls long before he reaches the top.

Retirement at sixty-five is ridiculous. When I was
sixty-five, I still had pimples. —GEORGE BURNS

Here's a man who may not do too much, but has had
a heck of a good time doing it. And he's certainly
delighted millions of people along the way.

George Burns has his own pace. You can tell by
the way he tells a story or a joke. He knows about
comedy. He knows about timing. He also seems to
know what is and isn't important to him.

Through my work, I had the good fortune of
having dinner with him about fifteen years ago. We
sat for several hours, which I found surprising, con-
sidering his age then and the late hour.

He spoke so calmly. He talked mostly about his
wife, Grace Allen. He told great stories, which is no
surprise, of course, but one thing I'll never forget
about that night is how even he was. No erratic
emotional outbursts, no extremes in his speech or
mannerisms. Just even, coherent conversation. He
was totally present. Not fearful. Not self-aggrandizing
nor self-pitying. Just wonderfully present.

.~.

If I could take a lesson from Mr. Burns, it would be
to learn to be more present, more aware, less intim-
idated by the passing of time.

Nothing succeeds like the appearance of success.
—CHRISTOPHER LASCH

I'm fairly certain that just because a man has a closetful of Armani suits and a Ferrari in the garage, doesn't mean he is necessarily happy. But, for most of us, those men certainly "look" as if they have it made, and, let's face it, most of us are drawn to that "appearance" of success.

But I think times are changing. And we're beginning to realize the sacrifice that goes along with all of those material gains. And more and more we have less and less admiration for the kind of self-absorption that's necessary to create this "perfect body, perfect car, perfect life" kind of guy.

Oddly, even those who still might want to "be" him would probably never want to be around him.

.~.

Today I'll be less involved in what I look like, and more involved in what I feel like.

It takes a revolution to make a solution.
—BOB MARLEY

We need to take total inventory of our disease in order to know what damage it has caused.

Once we know the extent of our sickness, once we get a feel for how we need to rebuild, then it's time for the revolution.

And there isn't a man I know who wouldn't benefit by the inventory or the revolution. Sure, we can slow down, take a day off once in a while; play with the kids, go for ice cream. But we know we're fooling ourselves. What we need is a complete overhaul, a period of releasing, of total evaluation, of honest down-to-the-bone reflection.

˙∾˙

I will do my best not to put a happy face on my work addiction. I will come to grips with the underpinnings of my disease, so that I can begin to rebuild and relearn.

JUNE 16

Nothing so needs reforming as other people's habits.
—MARK TWAIN

Well, yes and no. Having a habit doesn't mean it's a negative one. Some of our habits are good ones. But having too many of them usually signifies inflexibility and a need for order that is out of the realm of healthy living.

Of course, Twain is speaking of "other people's habits" like "other people's children"—we have trouble tolerating them. But we really need to look at our own. What do we do each day, each morning, each weekend, that isn't doing anything positive for us? Are our habits hiding behaviors and unfinished business? Strict, by-the-hour, by-the-minute routines and habits allow us to hide.

.~.

I'll look "beneath" my habits today and attempt to determine if I'm covering up unfinished, unattended business.

We thought, because we had power, we had wisdom.
—STEPHEN VINCENT BENÉT

How many times have we seen the wreckage caused by the abuse of power? Power makes us believe we have answers, all of them.

Power is an aphrodisiac—one that works on men, women, and ourselves. Our intellects and our hearts shut down, cease functioning, when we are drunk on power. We think of ourselves as invincible.

Power and wisdom are mutually exclusive. One cancels the other out completely.

⚫

I will be careful of my power. I will attempt to use wisdom instead. Then I will no longer need my power.

People tend to want to follow the beaten path. The difficulty is that the beaten path doesn't seem to be leading anywhere. —CHARLES M. MATHIAS, JR.

It's hard to know when to take chances, and what to take chances with. With the best of intentions, because we do value our relationships, or at least we know we should, often we'll use the same old worn-out means to an end, even knowing that we, among others, will probably be disappointed with the outcome.

Men who are chance takers and rule breakers are people who are less fearful of results. They are more concerned about the process than the outcome. And, as Dr. Anne Wilson Schaef tells us, we all live in process, we continue to grow, to build, to destroy, and one should be more courageous in taking "the road less traveled."

~

I want to be more open to taking chances and less resistant to trying new ways and thinking in new ways.

*Success is more a function of consistent common sense
than it is of genius.* —AN WANG

I know few men who are geniuses. But I know scores
who have long ago abandoned their common sense.
We tend to disbelieve that our first impulses, our
initial reactions, are of little value and are not to be
trusted.

We men who are work addicts do very little that
is consistent, unless you think constant chaos is consistent. We need to trust coherent, consistent
thoughts, and not look only for "brilliant" flashes of
intellectual fireworks.

.~.

I need to trust my line of thinking, my pace of
coming to a thought or to a decision.

If my doctor told me I had only six minutes to live, I wouldn't brood. I'd type a little faster.
—ISAAC ASIMOV

Brood? Who'd have time?

"Typing a little faster" has been the answer, figuratively speaking, for most of us. The way we make things work is to "type a little faster." Do a little more. Take on a new contract. Coach little league. Become involved in a new fund-raiser. We take on so much so often because, for one reason, we sense that time is gaining on us.

So we run as fast as we can, with few really well-defined destinations. The run, the pace, is everything.

~.

Today I'll choose to understand how much is enough. I will not push just to turn out more.

An appeaser is one who feeds a crocodile—hoping it will eat him last.   —WINSTON CHURCHILL

Most of us are appeasers. We're trying to please someone all of the time: our bosses, our wives, our children, our partners, anyone. We feel we're constantly being weighed and measured.

How did we perform? Are we good enough, did we do enough to be loved? Are we worthy of recognition from a tyrannical boss? Or is the "crocodile" us? Because in this mad rush to please, to be taken seriously, to be loved, we are the ones that are eating ourselves alive.

～．

First, I need to please myself. If I'm truly happy with who I am, and what I can do without jeopardizing my life, the rest will take care of itself.

JUNE 22

I believe in opening the mail once a month, whether it needs it or not. —BOB CONSIDINE

Men who do too much both anticipate and dread the daily mail. We know it may bring good news, sometimes money; but without question, it also brings demands and reminders.

Of course, it's the demands and reminders that stick with us, the part of the mail that stings and agitates us. Bills are expected, but how dare they send a second notice slip in the envelope? Didn't I already pay this? Or did I?

⌁

The consequences of my overcommitments are visible in my mail. It's time to take a close look at what's in all those envelopes and try to determine its relationship to my life.

I've never seen a Brink's truck follow a hearse to the cemetery. —BARBARA HUTTON

Maybe not, but there are a lot of guys out there who assume it will be the second vehicle in the procession.

Since so many of us have a major problem with denial—after all, we're not really workaholics, are we?—I think many of us don't understand when enough may be too much. There is a middle ground between living to work and working to live.

We can't take it with us; we need to enjoy it while we're here. Hoarding doesn't make you happy unless you've promised your heirs that they'll be rich after you're gone.

～

What is the money for? To enjoy? I think so. Today I'll begin to think of enjoying the fruits of my labor.

I'm a study of a man in chaos in search of frenzy.
—OSCAR LEVANT

I remember watching Oscar Levant on television when I was a young child. Even then he seemed to be a volcano looking for a place to erupt.

My parents thought he was brilliant, and I don't think anyone would dispute his genius. But he was the poster child of his day—a mass of insecurities, self-doubt, self-pity, and self-abuse, and all of it came across on television (even then)!

But Levant was and is not alone. Too many of us fill our days with frenzied behavior—and what's beneath the fervor? The feeling of isolation, being misunderstood, working alone and in the dark. Men who take on too much don't fail due to an oversized ego; they overcompensate for the lack of ego.

~

I will not cover up my need for order, for quiet. Today is a good day to look within for peace and reject frenzy.

Ants are so much like human beings as to be an embarrassment. They form fungi, raise aphids as livestock, launch armies into war, use chemical sprays to alarm and confuse enemies, capture slaves, engage in child labor, exchange information ceaselessly. They do everything but watch television. —LEWIS THOMAS

What an indictment! You'd think we'd learn about ourselves from watching a species that so closely echoes our behaviors.

I had an ant farm years ago. I learned all about their work, their systems and organizations, watched as they burrowed through sand making new inroads (that seemed to lead nowhere). They never seemed to stop and I remember wondering what they did for fun.

I still wonder if the ants have down time and I'd love to know what they call it.

•~•

I do not want to be just one of the ants. I want to enjoy my tasks and know that my work is a part of what makes me happy, and not some persona.

I arise in the morning torn between a desire to improve (or save) the world and a desire to enjoy (or savor) the world. This makes it hard to plan the day.
—E. B. WHITE

At least E. B. White knew the difference. So many of us either combine the concepts or arise only to work toward improving ourselves via more work.

I still believe that if we let ourselves enjoy, we can enjoy both. So many of us do not even allow time for enjoyment. We think it's the opposite of "production," of getting things done.

Today, and in the days ahead, I want to learn about the balance between work and enjoyment.

*The great corrupter of public man is the ego ... Looking
at the mirror distracts one's attention from the problem.*
—DEAN ACHESON

The problem here, of course, is that we're all "public
men," looking at our mirrors daily to see how we're
doing, how we're measuring up in the eyes of the
public.

We think we need to be political in our jobs. How
else do we get ahead, make more money, command
more respect? If we're politically savvy, and so many
work addicts are, then we can more easily get what
we want.

The thing is, when we look in the mirror, what we
rarely ever see is ourselves as we are. Our egos are
fractured into the hundred different pieces we put
out into the world that owns us, body and soul.

.~.

I will try to learn that I can think of myself without
thinking only of myself. I will try to garner the self-
respect that comes with working in perspective.

Every day has been so short, every hour so fleeting, every minute so filled with the life I live that time for me has fled on too swift wings. —AGA KHAN III

The days and nights grow shorter for those of us who do too much. Maybe the duration of our days is just right for those who are not so driven. Perhaps twelve hours of activity and twelve hours of rest is enough.

Because we do not know how to meter out our work or our responsibilities, we never have enough time, we always come up short.

The clock is not really against us. It is we who've declared war on the clock and on the calendar.

～

I will be aware today of the boundaries of time and let my work unfold during the workday. I need to observe time for myself.

Self-pity in its early stages is as snug as a feather mattress. Only when it hardens does it become uncomfortable. —MAYA ANGELOU

Self-pity comes with the territory. You show me a man who does too much, and I'll show you a man who feels that he's being cheated. Someone is stealing his time—his employees, perhaps. No, his wife. They're all plotting against him, driving him mad. How can he, one person, possibly work any harder? He just can't seem to do enough: the seeds of self-pity, despair.

What follows, as Maya Angelou tells us, is sadness. As time goes on, self-pity "hardens," making us unattractive, inflexible, morose, detached.

It finally makes certain we're alone. But then, we don't deserve to be with anyone.

⟋

I don't want the burden self-pity puts on me or those I love. I will examine why I lapse into that kind of debilitating pity the next time I feel it coming on.

If you let other people do it for *you, they will do it* to *you.* —ROBERT ANTHONY

While men who do too much need to learn how to trust, they also need to learn who to trust. If people disappoint you so often that you feel you can only "get it done" yourself—you may be choosing the wrong people.

It's also important not to be too harsh in your criticism. Many of us find fault in the work of nearly everyone. It takes time to know who can do it *for* you without doing it *to* you.

.~.

Today is a day to trust. I will keep both eyes open, while giving the benefit of the doubt.

Since nothing we intend is ever faultless, and nothing we attempt ever without error, and nothing we achieve without some measure of finitude and fallibility we call humanness, we are saved by forgiveness.
—DAVID AUGSBURGER

Perfectionism is one of the diseases we deal with daily. It comes with the territory; failure, we think, is always at our heels, and we're terrified by the notion of error or of being found out.

We need to realize that fallibility is part of the human condition, and we need to learn to forgive ourselves for being human.

✦

Today I will look at the mistakes I make as part of the fabric of the day.

Now here, you see, it takes all the running you can do to keep in the same place. If you want to get somewhere else, you must run at least as fast as that!
—LEWIS CARROLL

If you haven't noticed, the treadmill that most of us climbed on years ago has been overhauled, and its pace has been substantially increased.

When we confront our workaholism by thinking about making a change in careers, our first impulse is to run harder, faster. We think we can make a positive impression in our new place of business only by performing at an even greater pace.

If we change jobs, let us do so not only because the new job may interest us more or pay us more, but also because it will allow us to be more human. Let's make an effort to make a change that is a change for the better, not just a change for the "greater."

.~.

I will think about whether there is an equation between speed and production. It's probably an inverted number.

I imagine one of the reasons people cling to their hates so stubbornly is because they sense, once hate is gone, they will be forced to deal with the pain.
—JAMES BALDWIN

Dealing with pain is never easy. Some people cling to their "hates" and prejudices as a means of avoidance. Some, and in particular the work-addicted, medicate their pain with full calendars, committee memberships, meetings, and emergencies.

Work is our daily anesthetic. It numbs the pain of conflict, of financial loss, of failed relationships. But it also numbs our ability to feel and express joy.

Facing our own pain, evaluating our own losses and inconsistencies, makes us see monsters. Today I will be aware of the real monsters as opposed to the ones I fabricate.

It's not the labor that kills, but the small attritions of daily routine that wears us down.
—RAY BEDICHEK

The same old, the same old. It's an old saying, but it's often said.

Routine is a double-edged sword. For those of us who overcommit, it is a comfort, a set of accomplishments we can look back on at the end of the day and feel a sense of pride.

But a good routine is one that is mixed, that allows freedom, that encourages choice and thought, one that can scarcely be called routine.

Save for the constraints that most jobs and careers put on us, we should learn to live without routines.

·~·

I will vary my routine today. And I'll try to make changes in it daily until I do not feel a slave to it.

I would willingly stand at street corners, hat in hand,
begging passers-by to drop their unused minutes into it.
—BERNARD BERENSON

Clock watchers always scare me. Either they want
the clock to move faster or stop altogether. There's
never enough time or there's way too much of it.

But they're always aware of it. I know men who
can tell you what time it is, without looking at their
watches, and come within a minute or two of accu-
racy. That's frightening, because it means that while
the minute hand is sweeping past, so are their lives.

We should let our stomachs tell us what time it is.
We should not consult a clock until the task at hand
is finished. We should not superimpose imaginary
deadlines made of minutes, seconds, or hours on
ourselves or others.

❧

While I often wish for more time, today I will not
look at my watch at all.

We can become anything. That is why injustice is impossible here. There may be the accident of birth, there is no accident of death. Nothing forces us to remain what we were.   —JOHN BERGER

We humans have the possibility of change. That is what sets us apart from other species. We can reason, and through reason, we can make intelligent choices that lead us in new directions.

If we have trouble expressing anger, then we can reason new ways to cope and learn to exhibit our anger appropriately. If we find it difficult to be intimate with our partners, we can work through that problem and solve it.

We do have choices. But men who do too much believe the opposite. We think we are locked into situations. That we haven't any choices. That is a myth.

∿

I will not be happy with what makes me unhappy. I know I can always change, and I will take an inventory of what I want to change today.

It is difficult to live in the present, ridiculous to live in the future and impossible to live in the past. Nothing is as far away as one minute ago.   —JIM BISHOP

Living in the present, being present for ourselves and those we love is difficult for the work addict.

But if we recognize that life is nothing but a series of "moments," the past just a minute ago, the future just a second away, we will not mourn for lost days, months, and hours and we will worry less about controlling our future.

If we make ourselves aware of what we are doing, saying, and feeling presently, if we make ourselves "present" for others, we will find more value in our moments, our days, our years—our lives.

.~.

Today is a day of quiet reflection. I will reflect on how to be present, not mourn for the past or worry about the future.

It is much easier to be critical than to be correct.
—BENJAMIN DISRAELI

Criticism is easy for those who are disappointed with the quality of their own performance. Expecting more and more from themselves, they expect more and more from those around them, finding fault with the system, the workplace, the children, the boss.

Through the smoke screen of criticism, we set ourselves apart, but we may also be removing ourselves from the front lines of life.

Today is a day I will be mindful of my criticism of others. I will try to trace its origins.

The difference between being in a rut and a grave is the depth. —GERALD BURRILL

Men who do too much often find themselves in a rut of their own creation. The routine, the monotony of the work-addicted life-style slowly but surely replaces the desire to interact with anyone. We walk through the days, zombielike, fixed in our routines, locked inside our armor.

Part of this, of course, is self-protection. We think that if we just "stay on course" everything will be all right. We'll get wherever it is that we're going, and no one will ask much of anything of us.

But, as Mr. Burrill said, a rut is much like a grave.

❦

Today I will vary my calendar. I'll be more open about the structure of my day, and allow for positive possibilities.

How many cares one loses when one decides not to be
something, but to be someone.   —COCO CHANEL

It takes courage to be "someone" instead of being
"something."

For one thing, you have to expose yourself to
scrutiny, let the weaknesses show along with the
strengths. It is much easier to invent yourself than to
allow others to see you as you are. Flash the business
card, the easy smile, the practiced handshake and
forego the rest.

But, as Coco Chanel says, this masquerade carries
a heavy price tag. It takes great care to keep up the
front, and a great deal of dishonesty in order to hide
the truth.

Today I will be myself in all ways. I will not offend
those I'm near, but I will neither conform nor censor
myself in order to invent a lie.

The day will happen whether or not you get up.
　—JOHN CIARDI

We're all so important. What will happen if I don't get to the office by nine? What if I go to lunch and don't get back until two? Will everyone take advantage of me if I don't show up? Will productivity drop off if I take a vacation?

We're all indispensable, or so we think. We don't believe anyone else can make a decision, write a letter, or choose the correct stationery. If we're not stalking, managing, ordering, processing, the world will fall apart.

We've talked ourselves into this. The truth is, everyone and everything almost every day gets along just fine without us.

･～･

I will not be so self-involved to think that I am indispensable.

When you've parked the second car in the garage and installed the hot tub, skied in Colorado and wind-surfed in the Caribbean; when you've had your first love affair and your second and your third, the question still remains, where does the dream end for me?
—MARIO CUOMO

Never enough. The eighties, in part, were years dedicated to acquisition—it was a decade perfectly suited to workaholics.

In order to keep up with the social demands dictated by the images we want to project, we have had to work harder, faster, more efficiently. Because there's always one more try, a better house, a bigger bed ... but sooner or later, we all sleep alone.

~

If I need to have all this accoutrement in order to tell me who I am, I need to take a very close look at who I *want* to be.

Fanaticism is . . . overcompensation for doubt.
—ROBERTSON DAVIES

We call it "focus," "centeredness," "having a goal." But our singlemindedness often borders on fanaticism. And what are we covering for if not our own self-doubt?

We were never taught to ask for what we wanted —so we doubted ourselves. We were taught that everyone else's needs came first, so we doubted our own. We never knew how to confront our own questions, fears, and problems, which led us to be nonconfrontational with others, so we doubted ourselves.

We would not, cannot, and will never admit we are wrong, and this has given rise to the fanaticism that springs from self-doubt.

.~.

When we become totally inflexible and implacable, we are riddled with doubt. Today I will question what I believe, especially if it stands in the way of my happiness.

*Do not play this piece fast. It is never right to play
ragtime fast.* —SCOTT JOPLIN

We rarely listen for proper tempo. We never hear
the rhythms that nature, lovers, or composers have
created. We know one tempo—one beat: Fast.

We miss so much when we ignore the rhythms of
life. They're appropriate devices of timing. The tides,
a metronome on the piano. The timing of our heartbeat. Our breathing. We lose those basic rhythms
when we push too hard, promise too much, and turn
a deaf ear to the beat of our innate music.

.~.

Today I will not deny my body's rhythm. I will focus
on it. I will allow it.

The trouble with most people is that they think with their hopes or fears or wishes rather than with their minds.
—WILL DURANT

It is hard to clear the underbrush of our minds—the weeds of self-doubt, shame, self-pity, and guilt. We need to *feel*, not intellectualize. But we need to feel *clearly*.

Men who do too much make certain that their heads are as crowded as their desks are messy. The more we stack upon our psyches, the more we cloud the issues. We think with our heads, but our heads are unclear. And we transmit mixed messages like radio waves.

Today I will think beyond my fears and allow my thoughts to be as clear as my unfettered mind will allow.

We must not, in trying to think about how we can make a big difference, ignore the small daily differences we can make which, over time, add up to big differences that we often cannot foresee.
—MARIAN WRIGHTS EDELMAN

This business of one hour at a time, one day at a time is especially hard for those of us with work addictions. We want the whole pie, so that's the bite we take. We crave instant results, so we ignore what's good for the long haul.

We need to be mindful of the small differences we can make. We know only "large." We need to be aware of what "large" is composed of.

～

Today is a good day to make small changes—changes that, if maintained, will make me happier and healthier.

If A equals success, then the formula is A = X + Y + Z. X is work. Y is play. Z is keep your mouth shut.
—ALBERT EINSTEIN

We do a lot of talking. Commanding. Ordering. Bossing. Directing. If we spent a portion of that time *thinking*, we'd be far more productive. Even more likable.

There is a time for quiet. For contemplation. To cool down. To prepare for action or thought or diagnosis. Quiet often brings a peace of its own; a time to reflect, to strengthen, to forgive.

.~.

I want to inhibit my speech today. I want to find out what happens when I'm more introspective and less extroverted in my activities.

Wisdom is knowing when you can't be wise.
  —PAUL ENGLE

The myth in the mind of the man who does too much is that he is good or even superior at all he undertakes.

Have you ever seen an Olympic swimming champion also take the gold medal in the shot put? How about the expert mechanic at the Chevy dealership who's a neurosurgeon by night?

Knowing what you do well, what you do best, takes a wise and focused fellow. There are far more things that I do not do well, that I'm not equipped to do, than there are things at which I excel.

.~.

I want to be clear about my abilities; I want to begin making the right choices and not attempt to say, "Yes, I can!" when I know I can't.

The one important thing I have learned over the years is the difference between taking one's work seriously and taking ones self seriously. The first is imperative and the second is disastrous. —DAME MARGOT FONTEYN

We need to separate ourselves from our work. We need to know that when we fail at something, we're not failed human beings. This is the first thing we try to teach our children, yet it's a lesson we have trouble remembering as adults.

Our work is not us. Our work is what we choose to do in order to make a living. If we are lucky, and we have focused on our careers in the right way, we love our work. But our work does not own us.

❧

I want to enjoy my day, and that means I want to enjoy my work. But I can and will separate the two.

He who cannot rest, cannot work; he who cannot let go, cannot hold on; he who cannot find footing, cannot go forward. —HARRY EMERSON FOSDICK

If we let ourselves go, not entirely but in the ways we know we should, just think what we'll discover!

We need to learn to let go, so that we can get our lives in perspective. It is ironic but true that even though control is an important issue in our lives, we always seem to be fighting to get it back, because we're always certain we have lost it.

But losing control is sometimes necessary. When we let go, we learn what freedom can mean, and we have a new sense of personal power that allows us to go forward.

～

Today I will look for time to rest, to replenish, to gain proper footing.

Self-pity is easily the most destructive of the nonpharmaceutical narcotics; it is addictive, gives momentary pleasure and separates the victim from reality.
—JOHN W. GARDNER

We get into ruts of self-pity. And why not? We're overburdened by responsibility, emotion, our attempts at stoicism, and sometimes the only solace we have is our self-pity.

But we must learn not to mourn those things that we have the power to change. If we are honest enough and unhappy enough to confront ourselves, then we have true hope.

Self-pity is for those who don't see the need for change, nor have the intention to try to change.

.~.

I will break my cycle of self-abuse through self-pity because I know there is always the possibility for change.

*You are unique, and if that is not fulfilled, then
something has been lost.* —MARTHA GRAHAM

We see ourselves all too often as just a faceless number among the masses. A pair of hands at a drill press,
a computer screen, or a desk. Our identities, our
uniqueness is hidden from us because of our denial.

It is in some ways easier to blend in, become a
number, a nonentity, than it is to be introspective,
spending time to know who we really are, what our
goals are, what we honestly want. And demanding
that from ourselves and expressing that to those we
care for.

If we allow ourselves to lose our uniqueness, we
will fail in our quest to be at peace. We will always
find diversions that prevent self-renewal.

.~.

I have talents and interests that I do not tap into
often enough. Today is a day to look into myself, to
begin to feel some self-renewal.

*Happiness may well consist primarily of an attitude
toward time.*   —ROBERT GRUDIN

One thing we all can agree on: There's never enough
time.

But what do we do with the twenty-four hours a
day each of us is allotted? We rush, we push, we are
a blur of activity that leads to little except emotional
exhaustion and stress.

The view of time held by most Western cultures
is radically different than in other, older, less digitally
minded cultures. We think in terms of deadlines
(notice the first syllable in that word), and of finish
lines.

"To be continued" is a concept and a motto I
would like to see more of us live by.

~.

I will live today by my "inner clock," and worry less
about conventional deadlines and imaginary due
dates.

Don't be afraid your life will end; be afraid that it will never begin. —GRACE HAUSER

I'm now in middle age, and I'm just coming to terms with what my life should really be about, how I can change, set new priorities, think about how to attain peace, open up to others.

I've been afraid of death since I was a very small child. Death surrounded my life in certain ways, but it surrounds all of us in one way or another. But death—or finality, if you prefer—seems too often to control our lives, looking down, waiting to take us, maybe next year, maybe tonight(!).

Those of us who are work addicts have trouble facing death. It is, after all, the final appointment. So let's see what we can do to jump start our lives, to fully live the rest of our days—to open up to life and stop fearing death.

Today I will think about life and death in a realistic way. I will see my life as a process and think about the possibilities for the future.

Cannibals prefer those who have no spines.
—STANISLAW LEW

Bullies at the office (the playground of the would-be adult)—they're almost always work addicts. They mow down anyone or anything in sight. They eat their young, and they prey on those who may also be men who do too much and do not know how to say no.

Workaholics are often viewed as men who have great conviction, great character, steady and true beliefs. While many of us do not suffer from lack of character, we can, and often do, behave as perfect food for the bully cannibal. We allow ourselves to be pushed around, as pawns on their chessboard.

It is self-affirming to be able to say "no."

.~.

I will engage in an act of self-respect. I will have the courage and the conviction to know when to say "no."

For every fine, well-adjusted and smoothly functioning American, there are two who never had the chance to discover themselves. It may well be because they have never been alone with themselves.
—MARYA MANNES

Facing ourselves: That is what we're most afraid of. Terrified of. We'll run from anything that gives the vaguest reflection of who and what we are.

We are busy not discovering who we are. That is exactly what we do not want to know, and exactly why we immerse ourselves in our work.

We keep ourselves hidden in order to avoid pain. We must learn to be alone with ourselves, to feel the pain and the gain of self-revelation.

～

It takes great courage to be alone, and not fill up our lives with annihilating busyness. I will be mindful of that today.

The winner is one who knows when to drop out in order to get in touch. —MARSHALL MCLUHAN

Men who do too much are extremely fearful of dropping out. In our mind, that would constitute "starting over." But Marshall McLuhan wasn't talking about starting over—he was talking about making major life changes.

McLuhan knew that we often must walk away from what we know in order to create a new path for ourselves that ultimately will be more satisfying.

We have great trouble understanding that giving up is not the same as dropping out. The latter implies choice that comes with knowledge.

.~.

I want to concentrate on finding out what I need to know in order to get in touch. Knowledge will give me the courage to change if that is what is necessary.

*Money . . . is the string with which a sardonic destiny
directs the motions of its puppets.*
  —SOMERSET MAUGHAM

We get so involved in trying to assess our net
worth—not in terms of how happy we are, or how
at peace we can be, but, of course, in terms of the old
"bottom line."

Am I good enough? I'll just check my stock port-
folio, or make sure I've got the gold card. We never
look inward for our sign of self-worth.

It is a debilitating truth: We become puppets of
our work because our work makes us money.

～

Today I want to forget about the money I make. I
will not be a slave to my paycheck or look to my
wealth for emotional stability.

*Men look at themselves in mirrors. Women look for
themselves.* —ELISSA MELAMED

I'm not a sexist, but let's face it: Most men are not
too terrific at introspection. It may partially be cul-
tural, but from a very early age (perhaps birth) we
are taught that to look within is essentially feminine
and a waste of valuable time. ("What do you mean?"
you're thinking; "get busy!")

But if we don't know who we are, then what are
we? Rushing headlong, day after day into work without a thought about our self-esteem or whether or
not we're actually happy is a dangerous self-fulfilling
tragedy.

We need to see more than how our hair looks
when we look in the mirror.

⋅∿⋅

I don't need a mirror; today I will take time to sit
quietly to listen to my heart and pay attention to my
head.

*You specialize in something until one day you find it is
specializing in you.*   —ARTHUR MILLER

Where to draw the line?

If only we're happy in our careers and our work
truly fascinates us, feeds us, and keeps our minds
active and vigorous, that is wonderful.

The problem with loving anything too much—or
specializing in it, as Arthur Miller puts it—is that you
can get swallowed up in it. It begins to own you. You
become narrow. You begin to close doors, keeping
people you care about on the other side.

We know this, but it always bears repeating: Work
can be just like alcohol. It can kill.

.~.

I will think about what price I'm paying for my
career, how immersed I am in it, what it's giving me,
and what it's taking away.

The passion for setting people right is in itself an afflictive disease.   —MARIANNE MOORE

Even if you're not one of these guys, you've dealt with them hundreds of times.

They are missionary addicts. They not only do too much, they do too much to you. They smother you with (often) well-intentioned stage direction, they tell you what to think and when to act. Often these men are also religious addicts. With God on their side, work addiction is totally rationalized.

If you are one of these men, please heed the quote above. Look to yourself and think about why filling yourself up translates into controlling your environment and everyone in it.

～

Am I in control when I attempt to control? It's a very delicate balance. Today I will think about my compulsion to control others.

California is where you can't run any further without getting wet. —NEIL MORGAN

We're good at running. Mostly away—away from introspection, analysis, and inner-directed therapies.

It is more than a habit, this running away. If we don't have anyone to answer to (or for), we can keep the myth of being in control and being healthy and productive by disappearing. But most of us are not lone rangers.

We're hit-and-run fathers, husbands, lovers. We can't stay in one place too long, literally or figuratively, because we'll be found out!

I wonder if all those middle-aged blond guys surfing off the coast of California are work addicts looking for the perfect wave?

.~.

If I am given to moving about—from job to job, home to home, state to state, woman to woman—I'll examine that to see how it relates to my work addiction.

Success is a process, a quality of mind and way of being, an outgoing affirmation of life. —ALEX NOBLE

That's not what we learned in business school or at our father's knees or from the eighties or *The Wall Street Journal*. But you know that it's true.

If we look at our work as a portion, a component of our lives, keeping it in perspective and not hiding behind it or losing ourselves in it, then we have been successful in balancing and interweaving other parts of our lives with it.

There can be harmony between our personal interests and our work. We must be aware of how we can manage that balance.

．～．

I will investigate the process of success and what that means to me.

We do not remember days, we remember moments.
—CESARE PAVESE

When you think back on your childhood, you realize this is true. There are shining moments and blistering ones, but never entire days.

When we look back on our past, we do not recall it day by day, appointment by appointment, task by task. We remember the moment we first met our wives, the day our children first said "Dad," the Christmas the entire family was together, the Halloween it snowed.

Moments are what matter. Nuance is sometimes so powerful, memorable, life changing and life affirming that we need to record these moments, remember them. We must try not to lose them in a blur of frenzied activity.

.~.

At some quiet time today, I will think back to the moments of my life and think forward to what moments lie ahead.

We live in a nervous, restless age, ourselves fragmented as we glance at one another. . . . We are forced to see our own and other people's lives in side glances; we ask for the essence, not the paragraph.
—V. S. PRITCHETT

When we're doing too much and are drowning in our work, we have no time for one another. A vague "Hello, how ya doin'?" is as much as we can give or get. We haven't a minute for people.

We're like the big Hollywood studio moguls who ask for the reader's reports so they don't have to read the novels themselves. How much do we miss from the condensation of life's experiences? We short-change ourselves and create a joyless, dreary, cold place, but one in constant motion—always "in production."

⟿

I don't want to continue to see my life and others in side glances. I want a full faceoff with reality. I'll think of it as a vast adventure.

When a friend speaks to me, whatever he says is interesting. —JEAN RENOIR

We need to let ourselves be open to what others have to say. Those of us for whom work comes first are very bad at this. We tend to think that whatever it is we're doing at the moment is more important than input from another source.

We don't even think we're worthy of friendship. We see ourselves as worker ants, getting the job done. How could we possibly have the time to open up to a friend, to allow ourselves the richness and rewards of friendship?

Jean Renoir's quote is such a giving thought. By following his advice, we affirm ourselves as well as giving our friends the ultimate gift: our attention. We need to allow ourselves friendships and be big enough to accept ourselves in that role.

●～●

I do think about friends in my past from time to time, wondering what's happening to them. Today I will call or write an old friend, and try to let him know that I am interested in what he's doing and who he is.

The closing of a door can bring blessed privacy and comfort—the opening, terror; conversely, the closing of a door can be a sad and final thing—the opening a wonderfully joyous moment. —ANDY ROONEY

Knowing when to open the door is as important as knowing when to close it. Often we don't have a choice—our parents die, our children leave home, our job is given to someone else. But during these times we need to know how to close the door appropriately, and how that closure can help us open another door that may bring us untold peace, answer old questions, or invite us to ask new ones.

Doors are opportunities, and we should see them in that light. The finality of closing one brings the promise of opening another.

～

It takes introspection to come to grips with knowing about these doors. Today I will think about the choices I have, about the doors I have before me.

Good people are good because they've come to wisdom through failure. We get very little wisdom from success, you know. —WILLIAM SAROYAN

In fact, ask anyone who's had a great success to repeat it and you'll see how frightened they are.

It's not just the fear of being challenged to succeed again. It's because success is often achieved by happenstance, by mistake, not by design. And because it rarely takes wisdom to succeed, success is doubly threatening—there's no surefire map, no written guarantees.

But we do know about failure, and what causes it. If each time we fail, we allow ourselves to learn by the failure, then we have a chance for success.

People who are unafraid of failure, who view it as part of the process, can ultimately find the true measure of success.

~·

The next time I trip up, fail in some way, I will look at it as part of the mosaic that will finally help me compose my success.

Integrity is so perishable in the summer months of success.
—VANESSA REDGRAVE

We must be mindful of our ethics when we do succeed. Too often a new set of values, new morés more flexible than the ones we once adhered to, creep in and take over, and our integrity is lost.

We begin to believe our "press"—our constituency allows us a wide berth. Suddenly we are not so scrutinized as idealized. But we know this state of grace does not last long. It vanishes, and when it does, we are left half as strong, half as humane, as we once were.

Men given to the high that success brings fall prey to this predator. Our personal ethics, always a fragile code to begin with, are strained mightily when we sit high on the throne.

·~·

In my time, I have been successful at certain things; in the future I will realize that it is always successful to keep one's integrity intact.

The true portrait of a man is a fusion of what he thinks he is, what others think he is, what he really is and what he tries to be. —DORE SCHARY

How true. We are all a sum of intricately woven pieces—images we get from ourselves and from others.

And we grow and change. I am not on Monday who I was on Sunday. I may be better. I am trying to be. On Tuesday I may falter, but with the help of my friends and my higher power and my will, I will please myself on Wednesday.

And so it goes. We are components of so many things. Would that we could choose those components in the fitting room before we make our debuts. But since we are human we must be understood, not as constants, but ever-changing men who try harder every day to be better human beings.

⌒

When I reflect today on what I have done, I will try to trace each step—did I make my choices wisely, or did I think I had no choice at all?

Whatever the right hand findeth to do, the left hand carries a watch on its wrist to show how long it takes to do it. —RALPH W. SOCKMON

It always seems that our inner clocks, the ones with the pointing fingers instead of hands, are running about two hours fast.

Men who do too much never have enough time. And if we don't judge ourselves to be late, then surely, we think, others will gladly point out our tardiness.

The truth is, we are the ones who have the interior metronome, the one that's overwound, out of control. Everyone we know has the same amount of time in every day.

~.

Although I need to have a healthy attitude about time, and not use it against myself as a weapon, I will not judge myself at all today. I'll tell myself that time is on my side.

It is impossible to persuade a man who does not disagree, but smiles. —MURIEL SPARK

Those of us riddled with self-doubt are especially undone by encountering men who will not sink to our level. Not even for a little verbal sparring, a little demonstration of "who's the boss."

Sometimes the smile Ms. Spark speaks of is the smile of passivity. But most often, I think, it is the smile that says, "I have the power, but I will appear affable and let you think otherwise." Cruel, perhaps, but possibly a better, more clever kind of manipulation from a man who is in too deep.

·~·

I do not wish to hide behind a smile. I will be up front with my beliefs—not shaming, just direct.

People often say that this or that person has not yet found himself. But the self is not something that one finds. It is something that one creates.
—THOMAS SZASZ

If one is always encumbered by the feeling that there is too much to get done, too many people to please; if one is constantly filled with a sense of dread, a feeling that nothing is right, then everything is about 30 degrees cocked to the left.

Those of us who have had to fight to create ourselves, make ourselves new, as disease free as possible, limit our promises, and admit our addictions, know about Dr. Szasz's thought. We know that being passive and waiting to "find ourselves" will not work. We need to be full-time participants in the creation of our destinies.

.~.

I want those I care for to know that I consciously make my decisions, that I'm present for them and accountable to myself.

AUGUST 13

We have to learn to be our own best friends because we fall too easily into the trap of being our own worst enemies. —RODERICK THORP

Lapse; relapse; slip; slide; get up; start again. Yes, most of us recognize every one of these words and they mean a great deal to us. But how many of life's hard knocks are administered to us by ourselves?

We know how it is to be our own worst enemies. We know the shame of falling backward, the pain of looking at ourselves in the mirror. But many of us are also learning the joy and exhilaration of climbing back. And we know the value of building ourselves into that someone we can live with, that someone we care about, respect, and yes, even love.

⁓

Since I have to live with myself every day, it seems to me to be a very good idea to treat myself like someone I love.

Future shock [is] the shattering stress and disorientation that we induce in individuals by subjecting them to too much change in too short a time.
—ALVIN TOFFLER

It used to be called "manly" to adapt instantaneously to sweeping, dramatic change. Things change so rapidly, with little or no forewarning, that it is difficult, at least, for even the most sophisticated man to stay afloat.

Toffler uses the words *shattering* and *subjecting* because change is so often a force that comes at us without warning. But if we learn to stay flexible and resilient, if we learn that change and the way in which we adapt to it is not the end of our routines, but the beginning of freedom, we can welcome it and invite it in as a friend.

Often, "revolution" is just an overdue "evolution." If we don't make the changes, if we remain stuck in our routines, change will happen anyway and it will seem brutal.

∾

I will remain open to the possibilities for change, but I will be honest with myself about my abilities to survive a hostile, ever-changing work environment.

The greatest happiness you can have is knowing that you do not necessarily require happiness.
—WILLIAM SAROYAN

No one is happy all of the time. It would be preposterous, even childish, to think that we can be singing in the rain all day.

It isn't necessary to be endlessly happy. Happiness can be a distortion, another drug to take.

What may be more important than happiness is finding a sense of balance. When we let go of the notion that we need to live every day in Mr. Roger's neighborhood, we begin to grow, and to accept the defeats along with the victories.

.~.

There is freedom in letting go of the myth of constant happiness. I am now where I need to be, where I want to be. I am at peace with my process.

Nothing in man is more serious than his sense of humor;
it is the sign that he wants all the truth.
  —MARK VAN DOREN

The way we laugh, what we laugh at, and when we
laugh are things of self-disclosure. Our humor is
based on our needs, on our self-images; our humor is
deadly serious.

Men who do too much are often without a sense
of humor. Humor is suspect; laughter a time waster.
Humor, we sometimes think, is a cover-up.

It is also possible that humor gives us freedom. It
can enable us to deal with things that matter to us,
things that may be painful, distasteful, sad. Sometimes we need to laugh in order to say good-bye—or
hello.

~·

I want my humor to bloom. Laughter for me lets
down my guard, and lets me ask the hard questions.

During the 1960s, I think, people forgot what emotions were supposed to be. And I don't think they've ever remembered. —ANDY WARHOL

Andy Warhol was a great student of people. Somehow he knew, even back in the sixties, that people would begin inventing themselves to suit the fashion, morés, and general popular changes in our culture.

Now we are beginning to add emotional qualities to our self-inventions. We forgot for a while. It is hard to keep track of our own progress when change comes so swiftly.

Work addicts have long canceled their memberships in the human race. We need to accept our emotions and use them for reasons other than self-aggrandizement.

～

Today I will work to get in touch with my emotional side. I want to hear what I've been missing.

In God's economy, nothing is wasted. Through failure, we learn a lesson in humility which is probably needed, painful though it is.   —BILL W.

We acknowledge that much of life is painful. It is when we begin denying the pain, denying the reality, that we're in trouble.

Our work allows us to focus on something else— something that takes our mind off the pain. It is, sometimes, soothing; but it is always, first and foremost, a diversion that becomes our drug.

If we listen, if we pause, we can learn from our failures. Our failures make us strong, resilient, and giving.

～

Our pain is, oddly enough, what sometimes saves us. I will focus on that which is giving me pain, and I will learn from it and know it is a teacher with a profound message.

The large executive chair elevates the sitter ... and it is covered with the skin of some animal, preferably your predecessor. —EMILIO AMBASZ

Every business has at least one: the throne on which the master sits.

I remember taking note of the various sizes and shapes of the chairs of all the senior executives in the last corporation where I worked. The more senior the executive, the more elaborate the chair. A higher grade of leather; a broader, taller back; armrests made of teak. Each chair was different, all of them to some degree elegant.

Except for one: one of our younger leaders, a guy who recently had risen from the trenches, had a chair that had to have come straight out of a 1965 Pontiac Bonneville. He didn't care, though. He thought it was great. I wonder what he's sitting on now.

.~.

I know the accoutrements of success. And I know how unimportant those trappings are—emphasis on the word *trappings*.

I think anything like that—which is contemplative, silent, shows a person alone—people always feel sad. Is it because we've lost the art of being alone?
—ANDREW WYETH

Work addicts and men who do too much are people who can rarely be alone. Being alone often instigates self-awareness, thought, reflection, contemplation of self and those who we love.

Since we fill our days with activity, we are never alone. Aloneness brings us too close to ourselves, the very person we try so desperately to lose.

Only if we face our fear of being alone will we be able to begin our healing process.

～

Today is a good time to spend some time alone, thinking and feeling, not running.

I dream for a living. —STEVEN SPIELBERG

What a job description. What a luxury. Most of us do not live the way Spielberg does; most of us do not have the capacity to dream as he does. We have jobs and responsibilities that, frankly, require less of our imaginations.

But let's think about dreaming. If we deny all of our dreams, we deny what we *could* be, what we really want. Maybe, in some limited ways, ways that work within the realities of our lives, we should say, "I dream to live."

~

I want to hold on to my dreams, not cancel them, not dissuade them. I do not need to accomplish anything based on the dreams. I dream for the freedom it gives me.

They didn't want it good, they wanted it on Wednesday.
—ROBERT HEIMLEUR

Artists, writers, photographers—creative people in general—view workaholism differently than most of us. Many believe that an inner fire fuels their passion to produce, that painting a large canvas for twenty hours without a break is an act of artistic passion, not one of a work addict.

On the other hand, when art meets commerce, and has business to conduct, there can be a clash of great magnitude. Business wants it Tuesday, under budget and perfect in the first draft. Art says: I'm in process, rushing is contradictory to that process. If you want it good, it will come when it's finished.

⤳

I need to think about the clash between art (my heart and my head) and commerce (my need for outer stability and sustenance). I want to investigate the possibility of a balance of these diametrically opposed forces.

If a man watches three football games in a row, he should be declared legally dead.
—ERMA BOMBECK

Sports—one of our narcotics. We overdose on them especially around the holidays. Perfect diversion, the numerous bowl games. (This year there were no fewer than twelve football bowl games played between December 26 and New Year's Day.)

When we get caught up in the passivity of spectator sports to this degree, we really are in trouble. There are other diversions we need to investigate, like talking to our wives, children, parents, lovers, partners, friends. Like so many of our behaviors, numbing out in front of the TV is out of hand, too.

.~.

I will not commit to watching every sport ever televised. There are other, more important things to do, things that medicate me less but will make me happier.

We can always find something crazy to do in order for us to avoid doing what we know we should be doing.
—MELODY BEATTIE

Yes, it's true. Procrastination—avoidance—is part of the addiction.

I can make a list of thirty things that keep me from staying on task. Suddenly, I'm reading a book or magazine that's been sitting around for months. Then I need to get the car washed, and get to the cash machine—after all, I'll have all afternoon to get to the work that needs attention.

Most workaholics are great at inventing diversions. But avoiding the routine, running from the responsibilities, is not—I repeat, *not*—the same as freedom.

I will be more aware when I begin to wander, to lose focus. I will try to stay on task until the work is complete.

Don't confuse charisma with a loud voice.
—HARVEY MACKAY

You know the type (maybe *you* are the type): They're macho, they're noisy. They swear. They swagger. They holler. They demand. They appear to have been born and bred in a barnyard.

And they think that's "style," "charisma," "rough charm." It's a cover-up. The vibrato is an attempt to cover self doubt. They see the volume as manly, commanding. But it's the voice of a man who is always confronting everyone else, never himself.

Men who bully and bellow are men who are walking examples of the high cost of workaholism.

.~.

If I fit that description, I need to think about my self-esteem. It's wanting, and I will begin to try to begin a pattern of change.

I'm just not a memo writer. I like to look someone in the eye and say, "Let's talk." —PETER C. SCOTT

I like that sentiment. The memo is the paper trail of the workaholic. Although a cliché, I've often thought that a megalomaniacal memo writer was somehow justifying his position, covering his behind, and somehow believed everything he read (even those things he wrote).

I will not deny that some record keeping is necessary. But when you work in a nonaddictive, open atmosphere, a place where there are no tyrannical workaholics, the need for memoranda is nearly obsolete.

～・

I want to work in a trusting way. I must begin to make myself known as a trusting, caring, and up front member of that organization, and be the example of what I strive for.

The true leader is always led.   —CARL JUNG

I suggest that the most charismatic, the most vibrant, open thinker, is led by his heart. He doesn't trust the intellectual process. Not entirely. Sometimes not at all.

The true leader is a listener. He listens to those whom he leads, he notices who they are, he looks for cues in the themes of his people, he's aware of nuance.

He is no tyrant. He doesn't find his self-esteem intermeshed with those who report to him. He is spiritual.

.~.

I will allow myself to be open, to respond, to react to those with whom I work. I will not lead with my old patterns. They are abusive to me and to others.

Learn to pause ... or nothing worthwhile will catch up to you. —DOUG KLING

One of the reasons we workaholics have trouble remembering one day from the next, one month from another, without the aid of our calendars and a busload of assistants is that we make sure life goes by in a blur.

Our disease dictates that we do not pause. "What for?" we ask. If we pause, even briefly, it might lead to introspection. We might question what is motivating us, or worse, who or what is causing us pain.

The illusion of control dies out when we pause, when the machine we've feverishly built comes to a halt. Then we are left to confront who we are.

~

How often I've said, "Two weeks' vacation is not enough. I've just begun to cool out after the ten days, then it's time to go back to work." I will be mindful of the need to "pause" ... as the old Pepsi Cola slogan said ... to refresh.

We are all in this together—by ourselves.
  —LILY TOMLIN

Isolationism is one of the cornerstones of the work-aholic fortress. We have no intimate relationships because we trust no one.

Our work is our mistress, so our marriages and our other personal relationships are, no doubt, in a shambles.

Lily Tomlin's quote is valid, though. We need to be aware of the fraternity of workaholics, but we also need to realize that in order to change, we must first confront ourselves, not others.

~

Trusting others, learning to be intimate is a goal. I will think of ways to begin to be close to myself and those I care about.

I work as my father drank.
  —GEORGE BERNARD SHAW

The cycle remains unbroken. Extreme behaviors—
whether abuse of alcohol, food, sex, drugs, or
work—are all the same.

We see it demonstrated by someone we love and
trust, usually as children, and because our parent(s)
could never open up and discover us or themselves,
could never reveal themselves, show love, or become
intimate, but instead medicated themselves and hid
away, we learned the same messages.

Shaw's quote is as true as it is startling. We can
break the cycle if we are aware that it exists.

∿

I do not want to see my children grow up to be
addicted to work. I will do my best to learn to play
with them, to show them I am a person, not just a
drone.

AUGUST 31

Have courage to act instead of react.
—EARLENE LARSON JENKE

I think you need courage to do both.

We need to learn to react to the dangerous behavior we display, the life-stunting habits that have insidiously crept into our days and nights.

The courage to change comes from deep within, and it takes an enormous commitment and reservoir of energy to act.

We must take inventory of our lives in order to realize how important it is for us to act. First, though, we must react.

～

My work addiction costs me dearly. I need to assess the damage, and act to make necessary changes.

Your goal should be just out of reach, but not out of sight. —DENIS WAITLEY AND RENI L. WITT

When we subject ourselves to outrageously high goals, standards that only the superhuman can attain, we set ourselves up for failure.

We actually may reach that goal, but what we expend in making it ruins the victory. When we are obsessed with achievement, we are single-minded. And with that comes an abandonment of our values, a loss of self and a breach of trust with those we love.

Goals that make us stretch can be healthy. Goals that put us on the rack are ridiculous and cost us our lives.

~

One day at a time, one step at a time, one realistic goal at a time.

The chains of habit are too weak to be felt until they are too strong to be broken. —SAMUEL JOHNSON

Habits sneak up on us. Before we realize that our behaviors are being repeated, we cannot let go of them. These habits bring us some semblance of order, of place.

Habits also give us some sense of control. Then, when not checked or questioned, habits take over, and they rule us, and we no longer have control over them.

Habits are strong, but if we break the cycle of self-centeredness and perfectionism that helped create them, we have a chance to become whole.

∿

I will be aware of the myth of control, and take a close look at my habits. Do they rule me, or I them?

A camel is a horse designed by a committee.
—ANONYMOUS

Get a number of people together, with separate agendas, differing axes to grind and talents to flaunt, and voilà: you have an addictive, self-fulfilling failure, also known as a committee.

Democracy takes us not only into some strange bedrooms; the boardrooms can also be a little weird. If we only trust the "group," all decisions made by that group will only be as healthy or as sick as the sum total of its members. We cannot hope for anything else until we learn to design our committees to be healthy, nonaddictive places where ideas are shared, not a battle zone for dueling egos and a workaholic's theme park.

~.

This time, I'm the committee of one; I will be aware of how I react in group situations, and how I create my aloneness.

Nothing has a stronger influence psychologically on their environment, and especially on their children, than the unlived lives of the parents. —CARL JUNG

"What happens to a dream deferred?" poet Langston Hughes asks in one of his first, most insightful poems. He suggests in the end that dreams that have no outlet, wishes that have no possibility of being realized, don't just disappear—"they explode."

If we as parents deny our dreams, cancel our hopes, constantly defer to our addictions and our work, we carry on "unlived" lives. Our humiliation, our deep-seeded anger and frustration surfaces in many forms. Sometimes the pain of our dashed dreams manifests itself in losing ourselves in work.

Workaholics have many dreams deferred, and we leave a psychological slick on the beaches of our souls and of those we love.

～

If I do not confront my feelings and my disappointments, I am harming myself and those who trust me and love me. I do not wish to harm them, and in order not to, I must take a close look at the environment I've created by my workaholism.

Few great men could pass personnel.
—PAUL GOODMAN

We must allow for individual differences; give our fellow men and women a wide berth in which to express themselves.

Paul Goodman's quote is amusing and telling. Personnel tests quantify candidates for various jobs and professions. How do you quantify certain kinds of thought, expression, and indeed, genius?

You don't. You cannot. Instead you use the same tired yardstick for every poor guy who comes through the door.

How much work does he do? What is his production rate? Has he a high absentee rate? Is he strictly a nine-to-fiver? Will he fit in?

I believe most personnel departments should be called The Department for the Promotion of Workaholism.

·~·

I do not want others to use a tired, overly demanding set of criteria to judge my work. I will not do that to others.

Some people approach every problem with an open mouth.
—ADLAI STEVENSON

A massive amount of jabber, some believe, will conquer any problem. Maybe we can talk it to death, form committees and task forces to study and talk and talk and talk.

Sometimes the answers to problems are from the heart, sometimes from the head. Men who do too much talk too much, as though, by the very act of talking, problems are immediately solved.

Workaholics are not known for quiet contemplation, for reflective thinking. All too often we are ready to verbally leap on a problem before we even know what it is.

～

Today I will do my best to approach problems quietly, without coming to instant verbal conclusions.

Meetings are indispensable when you don't want to do anything. —JOHN KENNETH GALBRAITH

If you want to stall progress, or make a small problem into a protracted nightmare, call a meeting to discuss it.

I have seen good ideas and great creative plans practically disappear before my eyes when six or seven confirmed work addicts get involved. All of them zealots, they'll have the one and only opinion that counts, so sure are they of themselves.

If opinions rather than ideas ruled, we'd be in a bigger mess than we are. I never really saw anything truly creative or timely come out of a committee.

~·

I need to respect other people's opinions and ideas, but I do not need to call a meeting in order to weigh the relevance or importance of a concept or idea.

Learn to say no; it will be of more use to you than to be able to read Latin.
—CHARLES HADDON SPURGEON

Latin is rarely taught these days. Save for medical and law schools, it's nearly a dead language.

The word *no* is a word not used often enough by the work addict. We may be negativists, but since we're always ready, willing, and (we say) able to take on more and more, it wouldn't occur to us to say no.

When we have a full load, when our work and our lives suffer from taking on too much, we need to examine why we say only yes.

.~.

I know work cannot fill me up. And I know I must learn to say no, I cannot take on this problem or that project. My plate is full.

Don't become cynical. Don't give up hope. . . . There is idealism in this world. There is human brotherhood.
—GOLDA MEIR

Speaking of negativists, work addicts are some of the most negative folks one would never want to meet.

We are cynical because we are stressed, unhappy, unfulfilled loners. We see the glass half empty; we enter into few, if any, affirming activities.

Since we do not believe we're worthy of hope and we know by experience that idealism is folly; since we feel no camaraderie, no brotherhood, we are cynical to the bone.

We must begin to challenge ourselves enough to ask the hard questions, to begin to get well, to stop depriving ourselves of the positive parts of our being.

•~•

I will try not to approach life today as a cynic. I want to begin resolving my inner conflicts and stop covering them up under my work compulsion.

Take this job and love it.   —HARVEY MACKAY

We talk a lot about our work, how it encroaches on our personal lives, how it intercedes, takes over. That's because we let it; we have no clear boundaries.

Our jobs, once thought to have a stranglehold on our choices, might become enjoyable and fulfilling if we let them. We're control addicts, but ironically, we allow events, people, and our jobs to control us.

We need to learn to create boundaries; to walk away, to say no, and to say, "I've done enough today; tomorrow is another day." Then we can see our jobs in perspective and learn how to love them.

.~.

It is a wise man who knows his limits. Today I will see my job as one component of my life—not as my life.

I have received memos so swollen with managerial babble that they struck me as the literary equivalent of assault with a deadly weapon.   —PETER BAIARDI

We invent jargon to bolster our self-importance—to create walls with words—to keep some people "in" and others "out."

Newspeak, White House Speak, lawyerese, medical jargon, and finally, managerial babble. These are words and phrases that we all use and that come back to be used against us as weapons.

Jargon is an important part of any work addict's lexicon. We are comfortable with it, reassured by it. It makes us feel important.

·~·

I will make a very conscious effort not to alienate my fellow workers with verbal walls that I think keep me safe and aloof.

When I was a young man I observed that nine out of ten things I did were failures. I didn't want to be a failure, so I did ten times more work.
—GEORGE BERNARD SHAW

We are always our harshest judges. Our perception of our abilities is dim. We have the worst seat in the house, our vision is not clear, and we're the most difficult critics of our own performances.

So we push, push, work harder, faster, pile task upon task. Our self-esteem is never on par with our output. We've never done quite enough.

The problem may well be that we're trying to please a severe and unwavering taskmaster—one who never forgives, never forgets, never tolerates defeat. In this way, we let ourselves down because we can never forgive ourselves for our failures.

~·

I want to be kinder to myself. I do not want to create a mountain of memos that make me believe I've failed. I want to judge my body of work, not just my individual successes and failures.

Anxiety is fear of oneself. —WILHELM STEKEL

A good proportion of our anxiety stems from our failure to self-examine on a regular basis. If we could look at ourselves from time to time, judging not just the moment or the hour but the sum total of our being, we might be less anxious about failure.

And it is difficult if not impossible to assess ourselves appropriately when our expectations are too high. If we set an impossible goal, we are doomed to failure. Then we become anxious. We take on more work to counteract the anxiety. And the more work we load on ourselves, the more virulent the disease becomes.

~

I'm afraid to look within. I know there will be pain on reflection, but I know that in order to help free myself of this relentless tension I must see the reasons for my anxiety.

Trouble is part of your life, and if you don't share it, you don't give the person who loves you a chance to love you enough. —DINAH SHORE

Trust has always been an issue of contention for us. Men who do too much do so in part as an escape from intimacy.

And sharing is anathema to us—we feel it makes us weak or that by allowing another person into our lives we'll be found to be frauds.

We must take hold of our lives, allow others in, open the doors and windows of our souls and allow love and trust to provide the safety net all of us want but don't know how to ask for.

.~.

I need to share my heartaches and my headaches, and not always worry about taking care of others. There are appropriate times for me to be taken care of.

They intoxicate themselves with work so they won't see how they really are. —ALDOUS HUXLEY

We get drunk on our work. Like our alcoholic brothers, we have blackouts; we forget important dates and names; we have hangovers, exhaustion, health problems. We need the "fix" of work. It gives us the temporary illusion that everything is OK. It takes more and more work to give us that illusion.

From a distance, it looks respectable. But the disease goes deep—affects us at every level and makes a mockery of our lives and those we love.

~

I do not want to deny my life. I want to feel. I don't want the camouflage of work to keep me hidden from myself.

SEPTEMBER 16

There's a family on my back!
—LOUIE ANDERSON

We feel overwhelmed at least 110 percent of the time. It's not just our jobs. In fact, by the time we get home, after we've put a huge amount of psychic and physical energy into the black hole we call our careers, we're faced with the family.

The family. The wife. The kids. They all want a piece of you. I don't have anything else to give, you say to yourself. I'm drained. I really *did* give at the office.

Again, creating boundaries between work and family is basic to recovering from work addiction. When we come home, we should, as best we can, be available, be present for our wives, our lovers, our children. The family that gets attention is healthier; we become healthier and the burden begins to disintegrate.

·~·

When we give of ourselves, we give something more important, more deeply felt than any tangible gift. Today I will try to take time for my family—they are important to me, more important than my work.

Integrity simply means a willingness not to violate one's identity. —ERICH FROMM

If we have a healthy, integrated sense of self, an identity that we're comfortable with, one that we trust, our integrity is always intact.

Men who do too much often violate their identities. We do so little self-discovery, so little introspection, that we really have no identity. Our identity is bound up and composed of our work.

When we allow others to define us, our work to mold our lives, we lose our integrity. We have to build our identity, allowing ourselves to be who we want to be.

.~.

I am not just what my job description tells me and others I am. I am complicated; I am many things. I will try to be more comfortable asking myself who I am and who I want to become.

I don't like money, actually, but it quiets my nerves.
—JOE LOUIS

The fact that we need money is not in dispute. The realities of keeping a roof over our heads, taking care of the necessities in life are things that preoccupy a great deal of our time. To have "just enough" each month is frightening. To have a bit more than enough quiets our nerves.

But how much is enough? During the eighties there seemed to be virtually no limit on how much we needed. We need to rethink what that is, though.

Men who do too much usually don't have time, or don't make time, to enjoy the money that they make anyway.

.~.

What is my need for money costing me? Have I become "someone else" in the search for more? I will inventory my real needs as opposed to my imaginary needs. Then I will know how I can create my boundaries.

Few men of action have been able to make a graceful exit at the appropriate time.
—MALCOLM MUGGERIDGE

There is a time to go, to make an exit. Work addicts never think about this because we don't think about beginnings, middles, or ends. We live our lives on a continuum, a conveyor belt that never runs out of steam.

"Men of action" cannot make a decision to leave because they only know how to move on and on. They mistrust their internal cues; they do not know how to retire at the end of the day or the week or at holidays.

Knowing when to leave is every bit as important to our health as knowing when to begin.

～

I will not set an imaginary date for my retirement or a change in careers. But I will think about moving on, about new possibilities, about the second and third stages of my life.

Growth for the sake of growth is the ideology of the cancer cell. —EDWARD ABBEY

There have been a number of times, most recently the eighties, where, in this country, growth for the sake of growth did indeed create a cancer. The immediate rewards of growth at this artificial rate was power and a false sense of well-being and self-esteem. But look at what it cost us.

Failed banks. S&L bailouts. Bank fraud stock scandals. We created through forced growth a new decade of atrophy.

If we can use this "living model" of how dangerous it is to grow for the sake of growth, we can see how it can, and does, affect all of us in chemically dangerous, life-threatening ways.

.~.

What do I want? Am I growing to ease the pain of a deflated ego? Do I need an entourage of men and women to tell me that I am important? I will look for these answers in my heart.

Insanity is often the logic of an accurate mind overtaxed.
—DR. OLIVER WENDELL HOLMES, SR.

Overtaxed. Overburdened. I have seen men (indeed I have been one) with good minds; these creative thinkers, logical, sound intellectuals go slowly into the abyss of being lost, misdirected, lonely, overworked, overburdened extremists.

You can hear in some men's voices the vibrato of fear, the high-pitched fast talk of a man pushed to the edge. He is often alone. He may have had, at one time, a family, a group of friends who would have been his support system, but alas, they've disappeared. People cannot be codependent—they lose interest. They know that the relationship is only one sided, it's a no-win dead end. And if these men don't have something dramatic happen—a heart attack, a car accident, the disintegration of a marriage, an alcohol overdose—they spiral downward.

I will not let myself disintegrate. I will allow myself time to sort out my unhappiness; I want to live a more balanced life.

Man's loneliness is but his fear of life.
    —EUGENE O'NEILL

If we cannot or will not confront ourselves and our fears, allow those trips in our lives that we are most frightened of—meet them head-on and try to recover from them—then we continue to hide.

Hiding makes us liars. Hiding makes us lonely, and it makes us fearful. Frankly, it makes us emotional hermits.

Workaholism is intergenerational. If our fathers and mothers were work addicts it is almost inevitable that we are, too. We must confront this intergenerational illness. We must not fear our lives, we must welcome the possibilities of life.

∼

I want to learn how to question, how to open up, how not to repeat behaviors. I will concentrate on this today.

He sows hurry and reaps indigestion.
—ROBERT LOUIS STEVENSON

We all pay for our mad rush, our blind push, our hurried lives.

Work addicts do not get ahead by hurrying on and getting in front. They produce the least, have the highest absenteeism records, and have little, if any, job security.

We need to call a halt to the myth of the man who comes in at seven-thirty and leaves after dark. He is not "present," he is merely there.

Hurry gets us nowhere. Hurry is a cover-up, a myth, a mistake. And it's taking great tolls on all of us.

~

Slow down, I say to myself. Relax. The hurry to get to the next job, the next assignment, what does it do for me? Nothing, except it actually drags me down.

Men have become the tools of their tools.
—HENRY DAVID THOREAU

As a society, we have created a myriad number of tools with which to create, produce, and increase productivity.

The computer age (one on every desk, like a chicken in every pot), has made us efficient in many ways, but we now have the ability to create documents in minutes that not too long ago took days. The pace of our lives, due in some measure to the tools we've created to increase "output," has made us slaves.

We run from the fax to the conference telephones to the high-speed collating photocopier to the computer screen, and if we're lucky, with a stop at the microwave so we can heat our coffee.

.~.

I refuse to be a slave to things. I want to have only what I need. I want to keep it simple.

Most of the time I don't have much fun. The rest of the time I don't have any fun at all.
    —WOODY ALLEN

We can all relate to that, Mr. Allen.

Men who do too much don't have fun. Fun is suspect. Fun is a waste of time. It's frivolous. It's for kids.

We don't expect to have fun, and we don't deserve fun. We don't laugh much either. There just isn't time for it. Too much to do, too many appointments. Fun is small talk; I need to cut to the chase. Get my work done.

There is an inherent melancholia that is pervasive in work addicts. From a young age, humor was not valued. We learned this from our hard-working absentee fathers.

∙～∙

I will use humor every way I can in my work and in my life. It gives me life, and a moment that tells me not to take myself too seriously.

Two wrongs don't make a right, but they make a good excuse. —THOMAS SZASZ

Excuses. A real tool of the trade of the addict.

"Can't you see I'm overloaded now? How can I take on a new project? Four people didn't show up for work this week, and the computers are down. I'll get to your report as soon as I can. I'll stay late tonight . . . again."

When we say yes when we mean no, the inevitable excuse follows.

.~.

I will be honest about tasks undone. I will say no. I will be direct about my work load and I will reduce it. No excuses.

Forgiveness is the key to action and freedom.
  —HANNAH ARENDT

How true. And forgiveness begins with the self.

We must learn to forgive ourselves for our perfectionism, our total self-involvement, our inherent dishonesty, our need to control, our judgments of others.

Then we need to face our shame and forgive those who shamed us. We become "new" again when we let go of long-held grudges.

.~.

I want to look beyond my faults and the faults of others. I know perfectionism can be a prison. I will think about the freedom that comes from forgiveness.

One shining quality lends a luster to another, or hides some glaring defect. —WILLIAM HAZLITT

All of us are good at something. We have something about us that shines—something that, if we are fortunate, we use in our daily work.

We hope we get to use our good qualities, not hide behind them. We hope we are proud of our strengths, and do not regard them as a shield against our weaknesses. As workaholics, we need to learn what we do best, cultivate that strength, and do our best not to concern ourselves about what we don't do as well.

Mr. Hazlitt tells us that "one shining quality" can "hide some glaring defect." I prefer to think that if we develop our strengths we will never be shamed by our "defects." We need to concern ourselves with being human, being fallible, being real.

～

Today I will think about my strengths, revel in my "qualities," and not be shamed by my inadequacies.

*You have to be a bastard to make it, and that's a fact.
And the Beatles are the biggest bastards on Earth.*
—JOHN LENNON

I don't believe you have to be a "bastard" to "make it." But the overwhelming urge to compete, the seduction of huge sums of money, erodes value systems and can turn us workaholics into "bastards."

Some businesses are more competitive than others—the music business is one—and in order to "get ahead" we may sometimes find ourselves thinking of the prize, not the process.

Men who do too much sometimes leave their ethics behind when confronted with a room full of sharks.

⌁

I believe I can accomplish more, and be a happier, healthier, more giving person by not being an aggressive, attacking, demanding coworker. I will think about "making it" by being gentler.

*All the animals except man know that the principal
business of life is to enjoy it.* —SAMUEL BUTLER

Totally radical. Enjoy it? I thought we were supposed
to go to work, come home, think about work, and
then go back to work.

Men who do too much have a great deal of trouble
learning to let go. Our boundaries are hazy, and we
don't have a sense of self-worth that allows us to seek
enjoyment. We may medicate ourselves with sports
or television or a sixpack, but that's more about
passing time than enjoying it.

.~.

I will set aside some time today to think about what
I enjoy, and then plan time later to enjoy whatever it
is.

One's real life is so often the life that one does not lead.
—OSCAR WILDE

To an extent, when we give in to our work obsessions, we let go of our lives—we unconsciously believe that we have no control over the course of our days.

I know men who work as manufacturers' representatives who would be painters. I know insurance adjusters who would be musicians. Teachers who would be basketball players.

As children, we were never told to follow our passions. We were told to mistrust them, ignore them, they'll go away. And they do.

∼

I can retrieve some of my passions. I can find time for them. Today is the right day to rediscover them.

Avoid shame but do not seek glory—nothing is so expensive as glory. —SYDNEY SMITH

Glory is mythical, shame is not. Glory is expensive; it robs us of our time, and it turns us into imaginary emperors.

Men who seek glory need the cosmetics that it affords. And what are the means to glory as an end? Self-obsession, workaholism, isolationism.

Shame also isolates, denigrates, and erodes. It inhibits and makes us small. Sydney Smith's quote is a rich one, and we should reflect on it for more than a moment.

～

Today is a day to reflect on what I want. If I do not want glory, what is driving me? I need to know who I am and who I want to be.

I don't think anyone is free—one creates one's own prison. —GRAHAM SUTHERLAND

Workaholics are prone to create walls and fences, rarely bridges and tunnels. Because we are so driven to compete, compelled to industry, we are the architects of our limitations.

Freedom is achieved through allowing oneself to open as many doors as possible. But you can walk through door after door, rising higher and higher on the ladder of success, and still feel like a prisoner.

We need to learn to confront the limitations we've set for ourselves. If we're feeling like prisoners, it's because we're the wardens; it is a self-imposed life sentence . . . unless we take a hard look at what we've created.

The walls need to come down. I need to create an open life, one that is flexible. Today I will think about how I will make my life richer and less tyrannous.

A man is known by the company he organizes.
—AMBROSE BIERCE

As Anne Wilson Schaef and Diane Fassel say in their fascinating book, *The Addictive Organization* (Harper, 1988), when you take your disease with you into your organization (workplace, company, department), you replicate your addiction and create a totally sick, dependent organization.

There are millions of businesses, from Fortune 500 companies to three-man storefront operations, that are clearly addict-driven centers of workaholism. What we know about these businesses is that while many of them "reward" work addicts, the truth is that the work addict is the poorest, least effective member of the staff; he gives the least because he has so little to give.

.~.

I will be mindful of my work environment. It may be one of the sources of my disease. I may need to move on to a healthy workplace.

Never to talk to oneself is a form of hypocrisy.
—FRIEDRICH NIETZSCHE

The workaholic is not a man of inner thought and dialogue. We do not spend much if any time analyzing, weighing, or being contemplative. We're too busy making snap decisions, not trusting time or intellect to help us.

How many times have we thought that men who are highly decisive, men who can make decisions in split seconds, are the men we want to emulate?

If you think about it, it's fairly frightening for any man to always be lightning fast and so sure of himself. I have learned to trust those who think things over, who take time with a decision. Tonight's absolutes are tomorrow's doubts.

⁓

I want to be someone who talks to myself. I want to trust my inner dialogues. I do not always want to make instant decisions.

I am a man; nothing human is alien to me.
—TERENCE

And as Maya Angelou says, "We are more alike than unalike." We must begin to see ourselves as part of a global community, a member of a greater family.

Work addicts are well known for their isolationism. We set ourselves apart by seeing ourselves as harder, more dedicated workers—not prone to weaknesses, mistakes, indemnities.

~·

I am a member of the family of man. I am no better, no worse than the next man. I do, however, have choices, and I can make decisions that make me happier.

Anxiety is the interest paid on trouble before it is due.
—WILLIAM INGE

Work addicts are anxious people. We're not just anxious about today's various emergencies; we're anxious about problems yet to happen, about future catastrophes, gaffes, and failures.

Our outlook on life is bleak, our expectations low. If we were meteorologists predicting next week's weather, nobody would go outdoors.

Anxiety permeates our world, and we pass it on to everyone with whom we come in contact.

∿

I want to be aware of what is worthy of my anxiety and what is not. I do not want to travel through life as a forecaster of bad weather for myself or for those I care about.

Blessed are they who heal us of self-despising. Of all services which can be done to man, I know of none more precious. —WILLIAM HALE WHITE

Because work addicts have all the answers, they mistrust anyone else's opinions, thoughts, or philosophies. And if we don't know we're sick, why would we seek any kind of therapy that would make us well? We've created a self-image that is based largely on self-denial.

But we need to face the facts and get help. We need to join a group of recovering workaholics; seek counseling; read bibliotherapy; talk about our lives with those we are close to; let people in, turn our compulsion toward becoming healthy.

A session with a therapist can start the ball rolling. I will trust myself enough to try this method.

I postpone death by living, by suffering, by error, by mistaking, by giving, by losing. —ANAÏS NIN

Men who do too much think a lot about death. Maybe we're afraid we won't have all our work done when it's time to go. Do we think that we can keep it at bay by keeping busy? And if we're busy enough, if we have total control, if we just keep moving forward, we can postpone the inevitable?

Anaïs Nin took a different route. She postponed death, figuratively, by being so alive, so open to new experiences—by experimentation, by not hurrying through her days.

.~.

I will be open to life today and every day. I will begin to see risk as a component of the positive portion of my life.

Total abstinence is easier to me than perfect moderation.
  —SAINT AUGUSTINE

Workaholics do not know the definition of *moderation*. Neither can alcoholics be moderate drinkers; abstinence is what they must strive for.

Of course, we do not have to drink, but we do have to work to survive. We need to understand that we will be better people in all respects if we do not drown in our work; we must learn that "moderation" is what we strive to attain.

.~.

Saint Augustine did not have a regular job. But I do, and I need to learn how to pace myself, to make myself more productive and happier—to learn moderation.

You cannot consistently perform in a manner which is inconsistent with the way you see yourself.
—ZIG ZIGLAR

If your self-image is in bad shape or worse, if you barely have time to *have* a self-image, it will show in your work.

Work addicts attempt to cover their poor self-images by being compulsive in their jobs. Ultimately, though, because workaholics are less productive, more prone to illness, and more likely to create friction within the workplace, they begin to fail—publicly.

Losing oneself in one's work is just that—losing oneself. We must feel good about ourselves—see ourselves clearly—if we are to work productively.

~

I know I need to make changes. If I begin at home, with myself, I will be a happier, more productive person in my workplace.

*Some painters transform the sun with a yellow spot,
others transform a yellow spot into the sun.*
—PABLO PICASSO

Creativity. Intuition. Invention. Revolution.

Work addicts are rarely, if ever, people who will be described as employing any of the above words to their work or their methods of production.

As Picasso states, one can get the job done, but without brilliance, without imagination, without insight or beauty.

In order for us to do our best work, we must have room to grow, be free enough to transform the yellow spot into the sun. Living and working in that atmosphere is life affirming, nonjudgmental, anti-workaholic. Value is placed on invention.

~

I will assess my opportunities. I will think about how I can open up and be more insightful in my life and in my work.

Not seeing your father when you are small, never being
with him, having a remote father, a workaholic father, is
an injury.   —ROBERT BLY

Bly's concise statement is so pertinent to those of us
with work addictions. We know we repeat various
behaviors that we learned from our fathers—and
that, as Bly states, injures us.

If we are deprived of love, warmth, and a con-
nection with our fathers, we are bound to repeat that
behavior—we see value only in work. We saw our
father work ceaselessly, so we believe deeply that we
have no value unless we immerse ourselves in the
same way.

.~.

I do not want to pass along the legacy of the workaholic to my son. I will try to be accessible and
demonstrate my love to him.

The greater the ignorance the greater the dogmatism.
  —SIR WILLIAM OSLER

A place where rules, ordinances, and laws are prevalent is a place of total inflexibility, dedicated to ignorance.

If one is dogmatic in his thinking, instruction, and style of management, he demonstrates his limited abilities. Fear and ignorance are synonymous with dogmatism.

Workaholics are usually dogmatic managers. They run things *their* way, or *no* way. This kind of dogma breeds ignorance breeds workaholism, and vice versa.

~·

When I am *absolutely certain* of something, I need to question my inflexibility and make certain that my intransigence is not a symptom of my work addiction.

You must have been warned against letting the golden hours slip by. Yes, but some of them are golden only because we let them slip. —SIR JAMES M. BARRIE

Many of us work addicts are very sentimental. We mourn the lost hours and days that we did not spend with our children or our parents on holidays.

Workaholics often operate with our eyes closed. We don't see what J. M. Barrie refers to as a "golden hour" approaching. We see these hours only in our rearview mirrors. And then there are the times that all of us miss—the spontaneous moments—the great times when we've not *planned* to have a great time. We can miss them while in the midst of them. Our minds may be far away, our hearts not in communication with our heads.

.~.

I need to learn to be present for the golden hours. That is what life is—and those hours are the most life affirming.

In the nineteenth century the problem was that God is dead. In the twentieth century the problem is that man is dead. —ERICH FROMM

We constantly search for leaders, for answers, for relief from what can be long, difficult times. Work addicts do not tend to their spiritual needs. The very immersion of one in one's work denies deep spiritual exchange. Work covers up the wound, but it doesn't heal it.

Fromm's message is frightening. We have become a mass of men without direction, a group of work addicts who do not know how to trust our hearts or tap into our spiritual nature.

～

I want to be open to my spiritual side. I will be open to it, I will take time for it to define itself for me.

It is a mistake to look too far ahead. Only one link in the chain of destiny can be handled at a time.
—SIR WINSTON CHURCHILL

There are, of course, various "types" of work addicts. Not all of us are identical. There are those who are so obsessed with what is at hand that they are afraid to think of the "future."

But all of us do have one thing in common: the notion that we are able to handle many things simultaneously, believing that we can handle many links in the chain of destiny concurrently.

This is a mistake, of course. We need to develop a sense of pace, of timing, an inner rhythm; and we need to learn not to take the whole thing in one bite.

·~·

I will be aware today of my pace as I work, and the pace of my coworkers.

There are men who would even be afraid to commit
themselves on the doctrine that castor oil is a laxative.
—CAMILLE FLAMMARION

Commitment? Oh, we're great at commitment. We'll
commit to anything, everything. Just ask us and we'll
do it. Fund-raising for the orchestra? Sure. Coaching
Little League? Why not? Heading up the new super-
secret project at work, the one that keeps you missing dinners at home and taking up your nights and
weekends? Certainly. That's how you'll get ahead . . .

But in all that commitment, all those appointments, all the "doing good" that we do—aren't we
really running away from commitment, making ourselves unavailable, first to ourselves, and secondly to
our families and friends? We are, after all, totally
frightened by commitment because we see it as running in place.

～

I need to be more open, more willing to share myself
with others. I will look closely at what and to whom
I commit myself.

When we can't dream any longer we die.
  —EMMA GOLDMAN

Dreaming keeps us from despair, from loss, from the end of growth. It keeps alive for us the possibilities for change.

Work addicts rarely dream. We haven't time. We have narrowed our possibilities by succumbing to stress-intensive jobs. And when we do dream, we don't pay attention to the context of the dream. We don't believe that it is valid, that it could teach us something.

In fact, we find dreams irritatingly diverting. We do not understand what they can mean to us, and that we need them to survive.

.~.

I will begin listening to my dreams and will look forward to learning from them.

Eternity is a terrible thought. I mean, where's it going to end? —TOM STOPPARD

For work addicts there's never an end.

For us, the idea of an "eternity" is the endless sentence of sitting at our desks, or being on duty at the station, or getting up every morning at five-thirty to catch the six-thirty express train to the city.

For the workaholic, days turn into months turn into years of the same old thing—the long commute, the endless In Box, committee meetings, conference calls.

The workaholic may take time out to wonder if it's ever going to end.

~·

I will begin viewing time as a commodity, not an enemy, and not all to be given to my work.

For some time now, I have said that codependence is not just a relationship disease and that a good codependent does not need someone else on whom to practice his or her disease. A codependent can be codependent with a fence post. —ANNE WILSON SCHAEF

Or codependent with a job. And so many of us are.

We may know that our bosses are tyrants with egomaniacal tempers, that the quality of the product our company is manufacturing is inferior, that there's cheating and stealing going on at the loading dock; but, hey, it's my job, and I'm going to stick by it!

.~.

We have to ask ourselves, how much is enough? When will I be strong enough to detach, be willing to seek personal fulfillment?

Nothing is impossible for the man who doesn't have to do it himself. —A. H. WEILER

Workaholics love other workaholics, or love creating them. If I'm at my office at seven-thirty every morning, then by God, you should be, too. If I'm returning telephone calls at the rate of twenty per hour, why aren't you, too?

Delegation, we're told, is healthy. The sign of a good manager. But there's such a thing as overdelegation—where the entire organization has taken on too much, where everyone is stretched to and beyond the limit, all because nothing is impossible if you have enough coworkaholics.

∼·

I will do my best not to overburden those who work for me. I know we all need to set appropriate limits. I will respect them.

Suffering isn't ennobling, recovery is.
—DR. CHRISTIAAN N. BARNARD

"I suffer the most, and it's suffering that gives me character, that fills the days, helps define me." How often have we unconsciously thought that suffering is part of the burden of adulthood?

In order to recover, and ennoble ourselves in the process, we need to take a good, long look at our calendars. If we're overcommitted to the point of numbness, why are we? Who is responsible for the burden we bear? Suffering is a sign of sickness. The self-imposed agony does not make us better men, tougher, more thick skinned. Rather, it weakens and torments us.

．～．

I will try to discover what is behind my suffering. If it is, as I suspect, due in part to self-imposed over-commitment, then I will take steps to creating a more measured existence.

Why do men hate and despise the doubter? Because doubt is evolution, and society hates evolution because it disturbs the peace. —J. A. STRINDBERG

Workaholics don't have time for evolution, so they tend to force action. They create an answer for every question—even if it isn't the right answer. They let the status quo dictate progress, production, and movement. And they believe that anyone who questions—anyone who doubts the process—is suspect.

Doubters also create other problems for us. They may question the quality of our work or our dedication to our work. They may force us to question ourselves. We simply have no respect for those who take time to question the process or the product.

～

I will be more open to those who question, who doubt. In the end they may improve the quality of my job and my life.

Any idiot can face a crisis—it's this day-to-day living that wears you out. —ANTON CHEKHOV

My, how we like a good crisis. We like to stir things up if the day-to-day routine isn't a hot enough environment for us. We like an active stage, a lot of players, a great deal of noise.

But we'll settle for the nose-to-the-grindstone kind of existence, too. Routine is king when you're running a sweatshop or if you're employed by one.

If we repeat yesterday's "grind," self-imposed though it may be, we do indeed wear ourselves down. So we try to create at least one crisis a day. Maybe that's just to break the monotony of the other, more constant drudgery we've created.

Today I will break the cycle. I will try to find a way, other than crisis, to alter the stress of my routine.

Every new adjustment is a crisis in self-esteem.
  —ERIC HOFFER

When we undertake to make important changes, we must always envision ourselves—how we are, as well as how we want to be—within the structure of the change. Our self-esteem comes into question; it is challenged and tested.

Men who do too much don't want to call themselves into question. That is why change is so hard for us to deal with. We try to avoid shifts in responsibility, job reviews, changes in office policy, a new boss.

We almost always try to avoid the state of crisis that is brought on by changes—large or small.

.~.

We must learn to face change head-on, and not be immediately fearful of it. We must weigh the change and see how it may benefit us now, and in the future.

Compassion for myself is the most powerful healer of them all. —THEODORE ISAAC RUBIN

We are unforgiving in front of the mirror. If we make an error in judgment, we amplify that failure until an entire Greek chorus chants our downfall.

We must learn to have compassion for ourselves. We can begin by experimenting on those we care about. We will see a remarkable difference in the way they react to us when we treat them with compassion. It may take some effort, but the rewards will be astonishing.

Then we must turn that same open heart on our own places to be healed. When we look upon ourselves with compassion, we will begin to see ourselves clearly for the first time.

⋅∼⋅

Compassion is a component missing from so many person-to-person transactions. Its presence is felt and its healing power stays certain.

There is nothing noble about being superior to some other man. The true nobility is in being superior to your previous self. —SAMUEL JOHNSON

When we try to change, make ourselves healthier and happier, it is probably because we're desperate. The old methods have failed us or our health has failed us or our spouse has given us an ultimatum. Rarely do we come to these decisions on our own.

Nevertheless, we are there. At the threshold of a new life. We need to be clear about who we are in all the stages of our change. We will be superior to our former addicted selves only after hard work. And we will not gloat; we will see how far we've come by virtue of how peaceful we feel.

.~.

Superiority. A word not usually associated with recovery or self-analysis. Today I will allow myself to feel superior only in the sense that I am free of the work addiction that held me in bondage for so many years.

If I am not for myself, who will be?
—PIRKE AROT

In the end we are alone. We may have loving families, a devoted wife, a partner who is always in our corner. But change comes only from within. We cannot look to those people to make change happen or to keep us "new."

We must first be our own advocate. We must feel that we are self-reliant and that we own the choices we make and the outcome of those choices. First, we must take care of ourselves. So much else falls into place when we have been responsible to ourselves.

.~.

Many people may be *for* me, but my behavior can still work *against* me. Today I will think of ways in which to act as my own best advocate.

The cruelest lies are often told in silence.
—ROBERT LOUIS STEVENSON

Some work addicts seem passive. On the surface they don't show the characteristics we associate with the workaholic type. You look at them and they're not running, arguing, phoning, commanding—maybe they're even placid, almost peaceful.

But don't be fooled. Beneath that calm exterior, they're a cauldron of indecision, self-doubt, frustration. Their minds are racing, their stomachs churning. Their kind of workaholism may be the worst of all.

"How are you?" they're asked several times a day. "Just fine, and you?" they respond. They suffer in silence.

.~.

I do not want to be cruel to myself or others. I do want to learn to speak up and let others know I am in need. Passivity is not a cure.

When you are getting kicked from the rear it means you're in front. —FULTON J. SHEEN

Many of us are in positions of responsibility. We have a number of people who report to us, who may in turn have substantial numbers of people reporting to them.

There is nothing intrinsically wrong with being a leader. But leaders need to know how to take the heat—they need to know how to listen. Work-addicted men are notoriously poor listeners, and that leads to big problems. Powerful men, men who people follow and look to for inspiration and leadership, need to know whom they are leading. And why. What can the leader expect from those he leads? Are the expectations appropriate?

A leader needs to know not just that he's being kicked from behind, but *why*.

⋅~⋅

Today is a good day to begin the process of learning to listen. I know I have much to learn.

When we are not sure, we are alive.
—GRAHAM GREENE

There's a smugness, a dead-endedness, a finality, in being certain.

When we are certain, we're not open to new ideas or methods. Life is less an adventure and more an unending corridor.

Being certain, being closed, is not life affirming. Many of us work addicts are sure about just about everything. We're rarely open or vulnerable in any way; we do not trust intuition or others' opinions, we don't recognize our own need for flexibility.

We must learn that the willingness to allow other possibilities gives us life; it renews us and makes us a living organism.

⋅∿⋅

I will be more open to change. I know that it will help keep me fresh, aware, alive, open, and happier. And out of a rut.

The manner in which one endures what must be endured is more important than the thing that must be endured.
—DEAN ACHESON

I know so many men who come apart when they are confronted with adversity. First, they chastise themselves for not living up to what must be endured; then they blame others for "getting in the way" of their problem solving; and before long the entire situation has escalated beyond its original importance.

That reaction is, of course, merely another form of subterfuge. All of us work addicts are masters of "diverting the issue." But it's not just grace under fire that we need to learn. We need to understand what is worth noting as a correctable error and what is worth calling 911 to fix.

~

Today I will be careful to assess the damage before I use artillery to quell it.

Even a tax-gatherer must find his feelings rather worked upon at times. —CHARLES DICKENS

Some of us have jobs that are thankless. Instead of praise, we get the proverbial door slammed in our face.

If we have a position of that nature, and there are more of those jobs than you might think, then we must develop some rather thick skin in order to survive the negativity that is thrown our way.

It's especially important, too, that we take the time to acknowledge our feelings. If we can't express them daily—if indeed, we're forced not to express them at all—we might need to think about why we chose this particular job in the first place. It's probably true that workaholics are ill-suited to such careers.

~

Why have I chosen this difficult, thankless job? I will reflect on my reasons, and gather the courage to change.

Life consists of what a man is thinking of all day.
—RALPH WALDO EMERSON

Yes, and in the case of the workaholic, all he thinks about all day is work. And indeed, as Emerson suggests, work—the sum total of his day's thoughts—becomes his life.

We need to spend no more than forty hours a week with work on our minds. There are other things to think about: politics; art; family; religion; life.

If we think of nothing but work, our thoughts—indeed, our lives—don't amount to much.

.~.

Life and thought are one and the same. Today I will find a way to think about more than my work.

*Why are you feeling ashamed? Who have you
disappointed? Whose rules are you breaking? Someone
else's, or your own?*   —MELODY BEATTIE

Work addicts are fearful people. We were reared in
homes that taught us to "toe the line," "stop acting
like a child," "grow up." Our shame started there
and continues today.

We don't feel strong enough to create our own
code of ethics, our own morality. We aren't good
enough.

And we still are "measuring up." We cover for
our insecurities by working—ducking ourselves,
dodging our lives, and never knowing the freedom
that comes with confronting our disease.

．～．

Today I will trust my intuition. I'll feel good about
who I am, but also about who I will become.

Am I not destroying my enemies when I make friends of them? —ABRAHAM LINCOLN

We create enemies because we must blame someone for our mistakes. We create myths as well because we need to hear compliments more than we need the truth.

But since our enemies are the products of our own creation, we have the power to accept them as friends. When we learn to let go and back down off the barriers of blame that we've created, we can begin to see the realities of our lives—what is real and what is make-believe.

When we no longer need our "enemies," when they no longer have value for us, we can open our hearts to them. Suddenly, our self-imposed exile dissipates, and we can be whole again.

⌣

I've always needed enemies to blame—they've become convenient excuses for my inability to look within. Today is a day to let go of those "enemies."

My one regret in life is that I am not someone else.
—WOODY ALLEN

Men who do too much look at almost everyone else with envy.

> "He's so popular with women."
> "He's great-looking and active—I bet he's got a great life."
> "It's easy for him, he grew up rich, and he'll never have to work again a day in his life."

And so on.

The work addict always sees the other guy's life as the one he should have had. He views himself as a victim of circumstance. No one else has it as hard as he does. Life would be so simple, so easy, if it were "fair."

.~.

I have talents; I have a range of abilities; I can be giving and warm. I need to look deeper into the fabric of who I am and work on bringing to the surface those positive aspects of my being.

Americans hardly ever retire from business: They are either carried out feet first or they jump from a window.
—PROFESSOR A. L. GOODHART

The Puritan ethic plus a heavy dose of low self-esteem keeps us working way beyond our time.

Because our self-images are so enmeshed with our work performances, retirement is a truly frightening prospect. The workplace is a safe haven for those of us who have really never faced ourselves or those we love. We may wonder if those we've turned our back on for years will accept us now that we seek them out.

Of course, we "jump from a window" daily when we do not confront our addiction. We're committing suicide in slow motion.

.~.

I'm not going out feet first. I'm leaving at five, and I'm going to relax tonight.

If there's no dancing, count me out.
—EMMA GOLDMAN

One of the hardest things for us work addicts to incorporate into our lives is "fun." We think we're not really worthy of it, or that it's for people under the age of twelve. We tend to think it's a flat-out waste of time.

Our lives are in desperate need of balance. In learning what was important, what our roles were to be, we left the dancing part out.

A person can never be a whole, well-integrated human being if he denies the need for fun. And it is not fun to work every night until nine.

.~.

I will build time into each day for fun—a time to get away, leave the work behind me. I know it will be there when I come back.

He must have killed a lot of men to have made so much money. —MOLIÈRE

When our eyes are on the prize—whether it's fame, advancement, the corner office, or the greatest prize of all, money—we often lose our sensitivities to others.

We let nothing stand in our way. With blinders on, we forge ahead, ruthless and out of control. Our code of ethics, assuming we had one in the first place, disappears.

Many men rise to the top this way, stepping on the backs of other men to get where they're going. The most alarming thing about this kind of behavior is that in so many workaholic lives it is rewarded.

I will assess how much money I need, and I will think about how I will make it. It will neither be at my own expense nor the expense of others.

Too long a sacrifice
Can make a stone of the heart.
  —WILLIAM BUTLER YEATS

Workaholics have little to give at home. Our hearts have hardened; our emotions are either buried or tapped dry. Our obsession with our work has made our home lives unattainable.

We try to deny that this is true. Even as others—our spouses, lovers, children—are telling us that we're emotionally dead, we are busy denying it. But the truth surfaces and our addiction becomes apparent.

And regardless of what is asked of us, we cannot give that which is buried deep.

.~.

I must find a way to give those close to me what they really need. I will reflect on what it really means when I say I am giving to others.

Two things a man cannot hide: that he is drunk, and
that he is in love.   —ANTIPHANES

Or that he's drunk and in love with work. Or just
drunk with work.

When you see a workaholic deep in his addiction,
all of the signs are there: exhaustion, loss of temper,
lack of sleep, an inflated sense of one's importance or
abilities, sneak-working, hiding out, and so many
other indications.

We cannot hide our compulsive behaviors any
more than a drunk can hide his inebriation. And just
like a drunk, little by little we are eaten away by this
disease as we watch our lives come completely apart.

⋅∿⋅

I do not want to surrender my life to my work.
Being drunk with work will give me a lifetime hang-
over.

Most people have some sort of religion. At least they know which church they're staying away from.
—JOHN ERSKINE

Work and spirituality are, generally speaking, mutually exclusive.

Just as workaholism can and does take its toll on the body, it can also take its toll on the soul. When we are fully in our disease, and work replaces life, we lose all sight of our spiritual side.

As Diane Fassel says in *Working Ourselves to Death,* "Spiritual bankruptcy is the final symptom of workaholism; it usually heralds a dead end. It means you have nothing left."

～·

I will recognize the importance of reconnecting with my spiritual side. I have always valued spirituality, and I do not want to lose that part of myself.

If you refuse to be made straight while you are green,
you will not be made straight when you are dry.
   —AFRICAN PROVERB

Men who do too much are often set in their ways.

When did this happen? When did we learn so much, become so snug in our routines, that we began to feel that change was unnecessary?

To be green to change, to be flexible, is a way of remaining young, of giving yourself "more" life.

I do not believe that you cannot teach an old dog new tricks. The trick is to remain as green, as flexible as we can. Only then are we truly "alive."

∙~∙

I will be aware of how certain I am in my opinions, my promises. I will be mindful of the need to stay fresh, remain open, and be truly alive.

O! it is excellent
To have a giant's strength, but it is tyrannous
To use it like a giant.
—WILLIAM SHAKESPEARE

The arrogance and intoxication of strength is a fearsome thing. It is so easily molded into power, a sense of supremacy.

When that transformation occurs in the workaholic, he can become a monster, abusing his power and making life for those around him unbearable.

Ultimately, his new-found power works against him. He begins to feel he is, or should be, capable of much more than he is. He gets high on his own "greatness," creating myths by which he is then forced to live: I can do it all, I can promise anything, I can deliver everything, yes is the only answer.

.~.

I will not be a tyrant to myself or to others. My strength is in my inner light, my self-knowledge.

The proverb warns that "You should not bite the hand that feeds you." But maybe you should, if it prevents you from feeding yourself. —THOMAS SZASZ

Another kind of tyranny exists when a work addict tries to make his dependents grateful for his work addiction.

It works this way: I make it clear to my partner that the very roof over her head, the clothes she wears, and the food she eats are a direct result of my supplying them to her, and my ability to supply them to her depends entirely on my obsessive work style.

She thinks: Yes, that is right. I need your obsession as much as you do. I am dependent upon it. You become, in effect, my prisoner, and as my prisoner you never learn to provide for yourself, never learn to feed and clothe yourself.

Workaholism, in this way, provides a different kind of control to the addict and renders the recipient helpless, inadequate, and dependent.

.~.

My need to control extends far beyond my own life. I must examine my agendas and begin to discover whom I control and for what reasons.

To appreciate nonsense requires a serious interest in life.
—GELETT BURGESS

Work addicts haven't a view of a "whole life," a mosaic of experiences, people, and seasons. Our tapestry is sewn from the threads of our work—a daily total of experiences rather than a completed work of art.

In order to see life as a tableau, we need to stand back from it—as one would admire a painting—at a distance. And in so doing, we will undoubtedly see how funny we are. Maybe we can even laugh at ourselves, recognize the absurdity of our situations.

.~.

Laughter helps keep us balanced. The value of nonsense is immeasurable, for those of us who believe in balance.

*You've no idea what a poor opinion I have of
myself—and how little I deserve it.*
—SIR WILLIAM SCHENK GILBERT

Yes, it's true. We workaholics have a pretty low
opinion of ourselves. And we feel much the same
about other workaholics, recognizing in them the
same low self-esteem.

We don't deserve this poor self-image. You don't
and I don't. If we work to make changes, try not to
live beyond our abilities—if we are alive, thriving,
growing, moving forward—we can overcome these
negative feelings. And our lives can finally become
our own, even in transition and in process.

·~·

Low self-esteem is often at the root of work addiction. I'll spend time today thinking about how I feel
about myself—past, present, *and* future.

No, when the fight begins within himself,
A man's worth something . . .
  —ROBERT BROWNING

We are capable of growth. We can challenge ourselves. We can create our own happiness.

It is when we stagnate that we suffer. Then we do not know the joy of growth, the will to be better than we have been.

If we begin the fight—just begin it—we are alive, we are worthy, and we know that. To be alive is to be changing, questioning, realigning. Death comes in many forms. Never to demand a more than superficial life quickens the process of death. We are all worth fighting for.

.~.

I know I have the fire within me to evaluate what needs to be changed, and to stay the course.

That man's silence is wonderful to listen to.
—THOMAS HARDY

Workaholics are famous for commands, demands, and orders. We expect others to be as hard-working as we are and we let them know it—loudly.

It's as though we illustrate our worth by creating our own sound tracks. Work addicts don't understand silence and how it has the power to heal. We are so attuned to our own audio frequencies that we have lulled ourselves into our own addictive rhythms.

We need to go within, where it is quieter, ignoring the static that is all around us and that we have helped to create.

∼·

Silence does not mean inactivity. It may mean that I am deep in thought, and that I will be all the better for my inner journey.

The distinguishing sign of slavery is to have a price, and to be bought for it. —JOHN RUSKIN

Work addicts usually have a carrot somewhere in their view. Usually, of course, it's money, but it may also be power, prestige, or some combination of those things.

We never think we're slaves to money, prestige, or power; but, in fact, we see our self-worth only in light of the attainment of these things. Our value system is lead by the nose; we react to our needs as we perceive them.

But the price for attaining these goals is slavery. It's a high price, yet we're all too happy to pay it.

～

Self-imposed slavery is the most evil of all incarcerations; I will be clear about not wanting to be a slave to my work.

Yoga in Mayfair or Fifth Avenue, or in any other place which is on the telephone, is a spiritual fake.
—CARL JUNG

I know a lot of men who are work addicts and know all the jargon. They have an act that would, at first glance, make you believe that they are the very picture of focused and clear mental health.

Look a little closer and you'll see they're doing the same old things. They've just learned to medicate themselves a little differently, and their cover is a little better than most. They know how to fake it. They know how to "phone in" their spiritual side.

These men are cheating themselves. Faking spirituality is a kind of dual addictive behavior.

∽·

I know that I am becoming healthy, seeking my spirituality for *my* well-being.

Nothing recedes like success.
—WALTER WINCHELL

When we're addicted to success, to constantly proving ourselves, we learn the terrible truth: success is fleeting. Often its memory is cosmetic and a resource that helps to fuel the ongoing process of addictive behavior.

When we drive ourselves incessantly, striving for success, we can, in essence, never be successful. How would we know if we were? We're not even tuned into what we're doing, because our minds are racing ahead, formulating how we're going to accomplish the *next* success.

.~.

If we fully understand the process of becoming addiction-free, we will understand how temporary "success" is and how temporal it must be.

The resolution to avoid an evil is seldom framed till the evil is so far advanced as to make avoidance impossible.
—THOMAS HARDY

In the last stages of workaholism, just prior to death, we may finally realize how far our addiction took us. It is, in most cases, too late to do anything about it.

In order to avoid the finality of work addiction, we need to be aware of some of the most insidious signs of our disease: We cut off our friendships and become loners; we take on more than we are able to deliver; we abuse alcohol and drugs; we are afflicted with high blood pressure or other physical ailments; these are the early warnings.

If we pay attention to our disease in its early stages, we may be able to prevent it from claiming us.

·~·

I believe that I can change, that I can avoid the evil and finality of my addiction, but I know I must be aware of the signs of my disease and not fall prey to them.

The greatest danger of bombs is in the explosion of stupidity that they provoke. —OCTAVE MIRABEAU

Many of the men to whom I "reported," also known as my bosses, were men who dropped bombs—sent down edicts and made unilateral decisions.

They strangled and terrorized the staff, breaking our spirit, as we struggled to survive in an atmosphere of mistrust.

Many ill-conceived, poorly executed projects were the result. We feared these men. But we believed they knew what they were doing; the volume and force with which their commands were made often made us believe in them all the more.

.~.

I will question any men who are so sure of themselves and their decisions that they create an aura of unyielding certainty.

*The healthy man does not torture others—generally it is
the tortured who turn into the torturers.*
—CARL JUNG

If I feel good about myself, my work, the priorities in
my life, I have no need to display anger or throw my
displeasure in anyone's face.

It is only when I become totally absorbed by my
work, obsessed with it and overcome by it, that I
turn abusive, difficult and harsh.

When I am at my worst, it is my worst that is
handed down to those who are defenseless against it.

.~.

I know when I'm at my best, when I feel "clean." I
don't need to take my unhappiness out on others.

Life cannot wait until the sciences may have explained the universe scientifically. We cannot put off living until we are ready. —JOSÉ ORTEGA Y GASSET

So many of us work-addicted men secretly believe that once we've gotten our work done, once that report is finished, just as soon as Friday rolls around, there will be enough time for life—and, of course, there never is enough time. There are always things left undone, loose ends that need tying, one last project to complete.

We need to invest time in ourselves, for ourselves. Selfishly. Without guilt.

The climate will never be perfect, our calendars clear, our obligations finally met.

We need to make ourselves ready to live, to accept life, to be open to it.

.~.

I don't want to spend my days promising myself that there will be time just as soon as I complete ... whatever. I want to keep the door open and not fear what life will bring me. I know I cannot hide behind work.

It is an equal failing to trust everybody, and to trust nobody.
—EIGHTEENTH CENTURY ENGLISH PROVERB

We men who do too much have trouble with this issue. Why don't we trust people? Is it because we were led early in our lives into mistrust? Were we disappointed by our fathers, our brothers, our friends? Did we perhaps make the mistake of trusting those who could not be trusted?

Trusting no one can be as dangerous as trusting everyone. It is important to establish the bonds of intimacy so that trust is earned and not betrayed.

.~.

We must be able to trust ourselves, be honest with ourselves in order to trust others. I will be cautious, but I will begin to trust, and to know the responsibility of trust.

It is far easier to act under conditions of tyranny than to think. —HANNAH ARENDT

If we allow ourselves to be drones—to act out those demands that have been handed down by our bosses —we give up our freedom and eventually become the workaholic pawns that they want us to be.

If we can muster some self-respect and feel worthy of questioning tyrannous conditions and edicts, we are on the road to freedom from work addiction.

It takes great courage, concentration, and conviction. It is hard, and sometimes we will fail. But freedom from the slavery that is work addiction will make us men who are strong and self-reliant.

⋅∾⋅

I know that my workaholism has led me into slavery. I will fight back. I will be brave, and I will be free.

If you are sure you understand everything that is going on, you are hopelessly confused.
—WALTER F. MONDALE

I've sometimes felt that men who seemed to have a perfect understanding of a highly intricate situation were frauds. Good actors. At the very least, suspect.

This self-assuredness comes, I think, from a need to control. I've seen it in myself. In a meeting, even if I do not understand a given situation, I can spring to action and take command. This is a kind of cover-up; perhaps I fear that to ask for further explanation might be viewed as a sign of weakness.

The work addict refuses to show confusion or lack of direction, preferring that he be perceived by others as "perfect." Perfectionism is, of course, one of the mainstays of our disease.

᛫᛭᛫

I know that I have too much information. I know I do not understand a great deal of the information I have. I need to give in, not try to control. Control is fraudulent.

Pain forces even the innocent to lie.
—PUBLIUS SYRUS

The pain of being a work addict is matched only by living with and loving a work addict.

The person who lives with and loves an addict begins to change his or her behavior to cover for the addict. Women who love alcoholics, families who bear the shame of sex addiction—all the brave codependents who face the problem every day become a part of the fabrication.

We must learn that wherever we are in our cycle of work addiction, it is not too late to save ourselves and those we care about; we will stop the pain that forces them to lie.

.~.

If I will not change to save myself, I need to take a look at how my workaholism is affecting those around me. A hard look.

Unhappiness is best defined as the difference between our talents and our expectations.
—EDWARD DE BONO

One of the highest compliments you can receive is: "You're a real renaissance man." That means not only are you a forward thinker and you have a creative mind, but in fact, you are capable of almost anything. So many of us have patterned ourselves after that kind of "pop" expectation.

It's preposterous. Can Stevie Wonder do everything well? No, but he's a musical genius. Can Carl Sagan refurbish the Sistine Chapel? No, but he can see well beyond it. Could Martin Luther King, Jr. stop the war in Vietnam? No, but he gave mental ammunition to thousands who tried.

Workaholics need to stop expecting "everything" of themselves and learn to be satisfied with and grateful for their strengths.

.~.

The medium tells us we are men for all seasons. We are not. We are who we are. We need to be aware of who we are and not elbow others to define who we *should* be.

I hate victims who respect their executioners.
—JEAN-PAUL SARTRE

You know the guy, if you aren't him yourself. He's the one who, quietly and privately, condemns the man in the front office. But secretly he works twelve hours a day to gain his respect. He's a victim who calls himself a dedicated worker—a man who fails often, if not always, to get the acknowledgment he's breaking himself to receive.

It is a curious thing: a man who has so little self-respect, so little self-knowledge, that he's willing to stand on the assembly line for a tyrant because his picture is on the sign outside the plant. Why?

It is a form of masochism, of self-hatred, of self-doubt. A victim sometimes hides behind the master, never knowing who he could have been.

.~.

Our father may have been our first "executioner." We needed to love, to respect him so that we could, in turn, gain his love and respect. He became our model. Today I will think about my father and try to see him as a man with strengths and weaknesses.

*You see things; and say "Why?" But I dream things that
never were; and I say "Why not?"*
—GEORGE BERNARD SHAW

Indeed, why not? Are we really saddled with the
status quo? Or can we change the situation? Are we
talented enough, smart enough, to walk away, start
our own business, follow our passions? Are we brave
enough to listen to our dreams?

We don't dream aloud. By that I mean we dare
not give expression to our dreams. A dream might
force us to see that the question "Why not?" is a
good one. It might point us in a direction that's
altogether different—down a road less traveled.

We need to allow our dreams to be our wake-up
calls. Then, we need to ask ourselves, "Why not?"

∿

One of the curious, even paradoxical things about
workaholics—men who believe that they can do anything—is that we'll also settle for anything, essentially saying "That's the way it goes." I will not settle.
I will listen to what my dreams are telling me.

He's simply got the instinct for being unhappy highly developed. —H. H. MUNRO

Work addicts are unhappy and proud of it. At least you'd think so, looking at them. They wear their unhappiness like a badge—as if to say, Look at me; I'm so wonderfully "engaged." I haven't a free moment. I must be quite a guy to have such an impressive calendar. Sixty-three phone messages to return. Man, I'm something.

Our unhappiness defines our self-worth. But when it catches up with us—when there's no one left to corroborate our disease—our isolation begins to work against us. Our unhappiness has finally given way to total emotional bankruptcy.

．～．

Being unavailable to happiness is something that comes naturally for us work addicts. Today I will force myself to confront the emotional "vacancies" that do not appear on my calendar.

The best executive is the one who has sense enough to pick good men to do what he wants done, and self-restraint enough to keep from meddling with them while they do it. —THEODORE ROOSEVELT

So many of us are meddlers. We don't rely on the people we've hired to do the job; or we have no faith in our colleagues. We believe, without ever verbalizing it to ourselves or others, that we are the only ones capable of "doing it right."

When the inevitable crisis occurs, however, we find the right guy to blame. "Why didn't you call her back?" or "When did you make this decision—without *my* knowledge?"

We can't let go. And it's our death grip that finally will kill us.

❦

I want to know where to draw the line—I want to walk away from these things that I am not good at. I also want to learn to trust others to do the job.

A man who makes a big splash may be a man who has gone overboard. —PARKES ROBINSON

Most of us want to make an impression—the bigger, the better. We fantasize about proving ourselves in some "public" way. Some of us see our role models in people like Donald Trump, Rockefeller, Lee Iacocca.

We have never learned to be privately happy, to be content without fanfare. Adulation is important to us because we need to look outside of ourselves to confirm our self-worth.

We need to remember that Robert Maxwell also made a big splash when he went overboard.

∿

I am beginning to find happiness and contentment in small accomplishments, privately enjoyed. I no longer need a drum-and-bugle corps to confirm my abilities.

I find all this money a considerable burden.
—JEAN PAUL GETTY, JR.

Money is the tangible proof of our worthiness. At least we think it is. We live in a society that applauds the wealthiest. Why else would the annual *Forbes* 400 Richest issue be a sell-out on every newsstand?

We are known to some extent by the company we keep. At some point, it is the money that keeps us company, that defines who we are.

But Getty was burdened by his money, and said so. And published bios of the most wealthy, the most powerful, are not always flattering to read, nor do they portray lives that were enhanced by wealth.

~·

The burden of wealth can be as debilitating as the burden of any addiction. I must determine what I *need*, and not burden myself by working for more.

The time to relax is when you don't have time for it.
—SYDNEY J. HARRIS

Do firemen stop hosing down a blazing house to have a cup of coffee or take a walk? Since most of us workaholics are putting out fires, we can't stop. There's one emergency after another.

On the other hand, we must learn to relax and take a break. Putting out fires takes an enormous toll on us. Stopping to rest and to ponder how the fires started is important. Since we are pyromaniacs—in truth our work-addict behaviors start most of the fires—we need to begin thinking about how to stop ourselves before we self-ignite.

◆

Today, and for days and weeks following, I will take time to walk away, sit quietly, think about my process, and ponder my future.

My father taught me to work; he did not teach me to love it. —ABRAHAM LINCOLN

We were not taught to focus on what we loved to do, and then find a way to make a living doing it. What we were taught was that we should get a good, well-paying job, and that the company would take care of us after retirement.

Following our passions was not an option. Only rarely have men, as boys, been encouraged to follow a dream.

There is still time for most of us. We can renew the dream, strike out, and make our dreams work. We can love to work, to be involved with our passions.

.~.

As a father, I want to encourage my children to make a living doing what they love. We need to feel creative enough to allow ourselves to do what we love to do.

Nowadays, people know the price of everything and the value of nothing. —OSCAR WILDE

What are our values? What matters to us? Who do we care about? How do we show our caring, how do we indicate our values?

Men who do too much need life transcribed for them and delivered in shorthand. "Get to the point." "Cut to the chase." "How much?"

We've grown to know the bottom line of everything. But we rarely find ourselves in a conversation "about" anything, "about" anyone.

What if, suddenly, our families vanished? Our friends disappeared? Our mementos, photographs, diplomas, and private papers were burned? Who would we be, and what of value would be left?

～

I need to use this as an exercise. I need to be aware of my values. I need to imagine myself alone, without my work.

If you look up a dictionary of quotations you will find few reasons for a sensible man to desire to become wealthy. —ROBERT LYND

I have, and Mr. Lynd is correct. This book is full of thoughts concerning the burden of wealth, about how the quest for money is a disease.

I think many of us know that wealth doesn't really translate to happiness. But we still pursue it because the cash prize has become the justification of our work addiction. After all, haven't we already spent half or more of our lives in pursuit of the almighty dollar? How can we admit to ourselves that it wasn't worth it?

Our workaholism has us trapped into believing that we will find our self-worth in our checkbooks. When we really examine that notion, we know just how crazy it is.

⁓

It has taken me years, and more mistakes than I could count, to come to grips with the fact that my self-image is being dictated by my wealth. Today, I can finally see that this is a fallacy.

*Do you really think it is weakness that yields to
temptation? I tell you that there are terrible temptations
which it requires strength, strength and courage, to yield
to.* —OSCAR WILDE

Like the temptation to become healthy and fight
against our addictions. We need to be strong, not
allow anyone to detour us from striving to be healthy.

There are so many work-addict tyrants who will
confront us and try to get us back into their fold.
Our new temptation must be to work toward the
freedom that comes with controlling our destinies.
Facing the truth about ourselves, the unhappiness
and strife we've caused, is not for the fainthearted. It
will take an uncommon strength to change—and it
will take time.

.~.

I will do my best to replenish the fuel to change
every day. I will learn my limits, and in so doing, I
will learn that I have many possibilities.

One change leaves the way open for the introduction of others. —NICCOLÒ MACHIAVELLI

If we can begin to work in moderation one day, it will be easier to work in moderation the next day.

Change gives birth to change. Slowly. It is in our workaholic nature to make sweeping, sometimes devastating changes. The slow process of change does not come easily to us. We don't trust anything that takes time to complete.

But opening one door at a time is the only way to change old patterns. Over time, we will have accomplished massive change.

．～．

If I make one change today, I know it will give me impetus to make another tomorrow. I'll look for a new door tomorrow and the day after.

One of the reasons people stop learning is that they become less and less willing to risk failure.
—JOHN W. GARDNER

Failure is a four-letter word in the world of the work addict. We do not acknowledge failure, at least publicly. We hide it, we call it something else, we lay it off on others, but the one thing we do not know how to do is to identify failure, call it what it is, and then learn from it.

When we cannot or will not learn from failure, but we continuously fail, we begin to stop risking, stop giving, stop questioning. We become creatively deadened, or find ourselves in dead-end jobs.

．～．

When I fail, I want to face it. I want to know why and how I failed. I will fail again, but I do not want to end my need to risk.

He is most cheated who cheats himself.
—LEONARD DROZD

We work addicts are responsible for the world we've helped create. It's an odd place—an environment that is accepting of our crazy, life-inhibiting ways, a world where the only thing that seems to count is more and better and perfect.

We're responsible. At the end of the day, when everyone but us is left in the office and a profound loneliness begins to set in, we're responsible for that, too. We try and cheat it by not recognizing it, or by diving back into the wreckage of our work.

But let's face it. We've cheated ourselves out of what is good in life. When it is time for us to retire, we'll know we've been cheated—and that the cheater was us.

∿

I do not want to cheat myself out of happiness. I will work toward being clear with myself.

You can handle people more successfully by enlisting their feelings than by convincing their reason.
—PAUL P. PARKER

Workaholics do not work from the "heart"—they mistrust emotion. We are "head" people—all cerebral. A decision made on an emotional basis is not to be trusted.

The healthiest people I've known make decisions that are based on thought, reason, and emotion. This starts right at the top. A humane boss produces humane employees. I also believe that it is the key to happiness and peace in the workplace.

∙∽∙

I will listen to others at work. I want to know how and why they've arrived at their conclusions. I want our environment to be open.

The secret of genius is to carry the spirit of childhood into maturity. —THOMAS H. HUXLEY

Children ask questions. They are endlessly inquisitive. They lack adult inhibition, and so they learn and grow at an extraordinary rate. If given the chance, children will team up with others and create new ways to learn, to play-act, to discover themselves and their world. Theirs is an open-minded thirst for knowledge.

To "grow up" should not mean to "grow away." The sense of wonder, of spontaneity, of endless possibility, can be lost if we allow ourselves to work alone, in isolation.

.~.

The bully system will be replaced by the buddy system, the system that comes naturally to children who inherently know the "community" of growth.

*Experience has taught me this; that we undo ourselves
with impatience.* —MICHEL DE MONTAIGNE

When we are supermen—acting as if we were superhuman—then we make demands on those around us that are beyond their ability—not to mention their desires.

Of course, when those superhuman tasks have not been adequately performed, we become impatient, often saying, "If I want anything done, it looks like I'll have to do it myself."

We impose our workaholic behaviors and demands on everyone. Sooner or later, we end up in empty rooms, places cleared out by our disease, our constant demands, our impatience.

◦⌣◦

I do not want to be a man who causes the grief of others by imposing impossible standards on them and becoming indignant and impatient with their inability to cope with those demands.

Some people regard discipline as a chore. For me, it is a kind of order that sets me free to fly.
—JULIE ANDREWS

Many people believe that workaholics are highly disciplined people. Nothing could be further from the truth.

We may be addicted to full calendars, but the pressure to "get things done" makes our work habits erratic. We don't, for example, follow a schedule: work from nine to eleven, break for lunch, work from one-thirty to three o'clock, break for a walk, work from four o'clock to five. Instead, our work is haphazard and chaotic. We involve ourselves in whatever is at hand on our desks, whatever phone calls come in, whoever happens to walk into our office. Everything and anything that is going on at the moment becomes the priority.

ᳵ

I know discipline and boundaries can set me free. I can suddenly find time in the day for myself.

Everybody talks about wanting to change things and help and fix, but ultimately all you can do is fix yourself. And that's a lot. Because if you can fix yourself, it has a ripple effect. —ROB REINER

Good point. It begins with me. I'm my own worst enemy, but I'm also my own potential friend. Change can happen if I make it happen. I can even change the world, starting with myself—today.

If I undertake to control my work addiction, open up to people and their feelings, begin listening, curb my temper, limit my schedule, set boundaries, I know that not only will I have changed myself but because of the "ripple effect" Mr. Reiner speaks of, my entire environment.

Changes I make in myself will be reflected in my work environment and in my home; and over time, they will instill changes in others.

∿:

I want to be the first drop of water that initiates the "ripple effect" of positive change. That is a challenge, but one I can meet.

It is not the mountain we conquer, but ourselves.
—SIR EDMUND HILLARY

The mountain is us. When we set out to accomplish a massive goal, which is more important: the fact that we did accomplish it, or the fact that we were *able* to?

If we can conquer mountains, doesn't that tell us about our inner strength? If we can manipulate ourselves to create great things, then certainly we have within us the power to "let go," to break away from our addictive cycles of activity. Then we are able to find ourselves in the wreckage of our disease and begin anew, building ourselves into healthy, happy individuals—men who can make choices, not just take chances.

~·

If I am capable of great things, of "big" things, then I am capable of smaller but important changes. I need to see how I can conquer my disease and control it.

We learn as much from sorrow as from joy, as much from illness as from health, from handicap as from advantage—and indeed perhaps more.
—PEARL S. BUCK

We have the capacity to learn from virtually every life experience, but we must be open to it. If we see every adversarial situation as a dead end, a total negative, a lousy break, we're missing the other half of the experience.

Through the loss of a loved one, we may be able to see more clearly our love for another. If we lose our jobs, we need to reflect on why we did. Was it the wrong job in the first place? Was too much expected of me? Was I practicing my disease in the job? Was I addicted to it?

～

We can learn from adversity as well as through inadversity. If things always "went right" we'd never learn anything.

Be not afraid of going slowly; be only afraid of standing still. —CHINESE PROVERB

Bad advice for someone about to enter the marathon. But good advice for just about everyone else—particularly the work addict. To be introspective, measured, and thoughtful in making decisions—to take our time—is healthy.

But we don't trust ourselves to make decisions. As a result, sometimes we make them hastily, rushing through the process so we don't have to face it. Other times, we "freeze up" and become unable to make even the simplest decision. When this happens it may be because we are on overload.

We need to learn to pace ourselves, not to rush to judgment, not to freeze in indecision, but simply to trust our inner sense of timing.

~

If I am asked to rush into a decision, to come to a conclusion immediately, I will remember that it is critical for me to work at my own pace.

*Identify your highest skill and devote your time to
performing it. Delegate all other skills.*
   —RONALD BROWN

What I do best is most likely what I enjoy doing.
Since I am happiest, and most at ease with this work,
I need to learn to rid myself of many of the other
tasks that I am asked to perform.

It is no use trying to fake it. If I attempt to be
skillful at what someone else wants me to do—
something I know I don't do well—I will waste
precious time, both his and mine.

.~.

I must at least learn to ask for help when I need it.
I cannot be good at everything. I need to get onto the
things I most love to do.

Tomorrow is always the busiest day of the week.
—JONATHON LAZEAR

At the close of each day, I look to the next. Without really analyzing why, I believe that tomorrow will give me enough time to finish all of what I was unable to do today, and that tomorrow's ten hours will be the answer to today's exhausted clock.

I have for so long been negative about "tomorrow," dreading it, knowing that all that was not accomplished today, yesterday, and the day before falls on the shoulders of tomorrow.

~

I need to stop looking toward tomorrow. I need to look at the entire week, month, and year. There are many days ahead to get the appropriate amount of work finished. Tomorrow will be busy, but only as busy as I let it be.

Wealth can't buy health, but health can buy wealth.
—HENRY DAVID THOREAU

One of the things workaholics ignore is their health; conversely, one of the things workaholics are highly attentive to is their wealth.

Among workaholics, there is a very high rate of hypertension, alcoholism, chronic fatigue syndrome, sexually transmitted diseases, and numerous other chronic ailments.

After we've driven ourselves literally into the ground, we see the error in our ways. It may be nearly too late to do anything about it; but a chronic illness can blow the whistle on our work addiction.

We must be willing to pay attention to our bodies, and not ignore all the warning signs they give us.

～

When I am physically healthy, I am especially alert, I have great stamina, and work does not "inflict" itself on me. Today I will think about the messages my body is sending me.

Workaholics commit slow suicide by refusing to allow the child inside them to play.
—DR. LAURENCE SUSSER

I have seen men who only very reluctantly will even take in a movie. Once they get to the theater, they often fall asleep, missing the movie altogether.

Maybe we don't acknowledge "the child inside" because we have never been children. Most of us were robbed of our childhoods, so we don't know how to be spontaneous—childlike. We don't know how to play.

We need to tap into this valuable resource. There is a child in each of us just waiting to be set free.

·~·

I will feel free enough to experiment. I want to foster a child within. I want to see what it means to be free, to have the heart of a child.

A man must learn to forgive himself.
—ARTHUR DAVISON FICKE

Our self-ridicule goes deep. We learned from child-hood on to be harsh judges of ourselves, fearing intimacy because we were not worthy of love.

First we must learn to let go of the past; we must learn how to forgive ourselves so that we can move forward in our lives.

If a man can forgive himself, he will know how to forgive others, and not to rely on past truths or past failures. He can begin anew.

～

Mistakes have been made. I have misjudged, not allowed anyone in my life. I have acted alone. I will begin to learn to let go, to forgive myself.

To everything there is a season, and a time to every purpose under heaven; A time to be born, and a time to die; a time to plant, and a time to pluck up that which is planted. —ECCLESIASTES 3:1–2

Work addicts are shocked by the notion of "seasonality." To us there is only one season—the season to work, to get things done. Any time is the right time to get something done. No time is the right time to rest, to harvest the crop that our work has grown for us.

We can no more accept seasons than we can accept an eight-hour day. We know only how to labor; but we are missing the fruits of our labor.

.~.

Life is not endless. We have a limited time to enjoy our families, our children, our friends and our jobs. There are many seasons; I will experience them all.

Because it is less structured than work, leisure time leaves
workaholics at a loss for what to do. Workaholics
practically climb the wall when they can't work.
—MARILYN MACHOLOWITZ

Go to any resort, good hotel, or even an airport lounge.
The guys on the phones are the addicts. They need to
check into the office every chance they get, because in
their absence the entire business might evaporate.

Cut to the pool: The work addict has *The Wall
Street Journal, The New York Times,* a spy thriller, a
Hertz or Avis map of the area, a Sony Walkman,
sunblock, and a phone(!). The work addict rarely gets
wet unless he's splashed by an unthinking child. If
the phone next to him is in use, he'll worry and fret
until he's paged to pick up the house phone.

A scene from a family car trip: "No, honey, I know
we can make it all the way to Minneapolis by tonight
if we don't stop for dinner. The kids? They can fall
asleep in the back."

Waiting for a table: "Well, do you have anything
in the smoking section? No, I don't smoke, but we're
in a hurry!"

～

This sounds too familiar. This year I will try not to
rush through my leisure time. I will think of my fam
ily and friends—those around me who are waiting
for me to be a whole person.

REFERENCES

In the creation of this book, the following books were of great value and guidance:

Escape from Intimacy: Untangling the "Love" Addictions: Sex, Romance, and Relationships (San Francisco: Harper & Row, 1989), by Anne Wilson Schaef.

Simpson's Contemporary Quotations: The Most Notable Quotes Since 1950 (Boston: Houghton Mifflin Co., 1988), compiled by James B. Simpson. Foreword by Daniel J. Boorstin.

At My Father's Wedding: Reclaiming Our True Masculinity (New York: Bantam Books, 1991), by John Lee.

Father: The Figure and the Force (New York: Warner Books, 1974), by Christopher P. Andersen.

Meditations for Women Who Do Too Much (San Francisco: Harper & Row, 1990), by Anne Wilson Schaef.

Men and Feelings: Understanding the Male Experience (Deerfield Beach, Fla.: Health Communications, Inc., 1991), by David J. Kundz.

1,911 Best Things Anybody Ever Said (New York: Fawcett Columbine Books, 1988), compiled by Robert Byrne.

Codependent No More: How to Stop Controlling Others and Start Caring for Yourself (San Francisco: Harper/Hazelden, 1987), by Melody Beattie.

Working Ourselves to Death: The High Cost of Workaholism and the Rewards of Recovery (San Francisco:

Harper San Francisco, 1990), by Diane Fassel.

Best Quotations for All Occasions (New York: Fawcett Premier, 1990), arranged and edited by Lewis C. Henry.

Power Quotes (Detroit: Visible Ink Press, 1992), compiled by Daniel B. Baker.

The Oxford Dictionary of Modern Quotations (New York: Oxford University Press, 1991), edited by Tony Augarde.

Bartlett's Familiar Quotations (Boston: Little, Brown & Co., 1980), compiled by John Bartlett.

A Treasury of Business Quotations (New York: Ballantine Books, 1990), compiled by Michael C. Thorsett.

Speaker's Library of Business Stories, Anecdotes and Humor (Englewood Cliffs, N.J.; Prentice Hall Press, 1990), compiled by Joe Griffith.

The Addictive Organization (San Francisco: Harper San Francisco, 1988), by Anne Wilson Schaef and Diane Fassel.

The Language of Letting Go (San Francisco: Harper/Hazelden, 1990), by Melody Beattie.

Quotations of Wit and Wisdom (New York: W. W. Norton, 1975), compiled by John W. Gardner and Francesca G. Reese.

The Concise Columbia Dictionary of Quotations (New York: Avon Books, 1989), compiled by Robert Andrews.

Barnes & Noble Book of Quotations (New York: Harper Perennial, 1987), edited by Robert I. Fitzeray.

INDEX